Philip R. Stone

111 Dark Places in Scotland That You Shouldn't Miss

111

emons:

For my siblings:
David, Susan, Stephen, Elisabeth and Rachel
Fratres et sorores

Bibliographical information of the Deutsche Nationalbibliothek
The Deutsche Nationalbibliothek lists this publication in
the Deutsche Nationalbibliografie; detailed bibliographical data
are available on the internet at http://dnb.d-nb.de.

MIX
Paper | Supporting responsible forestry
FSC® C043106

Cäcilienstraße 48, 50667 Köln
info@emons-verlag.de

Layout: Eva Kraskes, based on a design
by Lübbeke | Naumann | Thoben
Maps: altancicek.design, www.altancicek.de
Basic cartographical information from Openstreetmap,
© OpenStreetMap-Mitwirkende, OdbL
Edited by: Ros Horton
Printing and binding: Grafisches Centrum Cuno, Calbe
Printed in Germany 2025
ISBN 978-3-7408-1895-1
First edition

Guidebooks for Locals & Experienced Travellers
Join us in uncovering new places around the world at
www.111places.com

Foreword

We live in a dominion of the dead. With sites of remembrance, our noteworthy deceased are scattered throughout touristic landscapes. Yet, commemoration of the significant dead is often contested, and 'heritage that hurts' is imbued with politics of remembrance. As a proud and strong country within the United Kingdom, Scotland often calls upon it's symbolic departed to give credence to its national identity and to serve as a warning for the future. This visitation to sites of momentous death, disaster, or the macabre is known as 'dark tourism'.

In Scotland, a country born out of turmoil with its dominant neighbour, England, many places are associated with cultural trauma. Indeed, battlefields of yesteryear have shaped Scottish nationhood, with the bloody carnage of the past influencing modern-day 'Scottishness'. Other sites, associated with rebellious acts or the casualties of religious bigotry or political persecution, are integral to Scottish dark tourism. Moreover, victims and villains from Scotland's tragic past, often obscured by time, offer us counsel regarding our own modern fights, follies, and misfortunes.

This guidebook will take you to places of 'pain and shame', as well as sites of difficult heritage throughout Scotland. From the Borders to the Highlands and Islands, this book will allow you to explore the history of Scottish places associated with fatality and spaces of ruination or forgotten traumascapes. However, as you engage in dark tourism, you are not a 'dark' tourist, but merely someone interested in understanding your own sense of being in a fragmented world built upon a turbulent past. As our significant dead become spectacular in a society that values spectacle, this unique guidebook permits you to sightsee in the mansions of the departed. As you do, have reverence for those who came before us and heed the messages each 'dark place' can impart.

111 Dark Places

SOLDIER'S LEAP

1 Hermitage Castle

Guardhouse of the 'bloodiest' valley in Britain

On windswept moors that border Scotland and England stands a foreboding castle. Hermitage Castle is an eerie place known as the guardhouse of the 'bloodiest' valley in Britain. Situated in a region that saw many violent struggles, border reivers roamed from the late 13th to early 17th centuries. With a predatory way of living, reivers raided communities regardless of victims' nationality.

Hermitage Castle has an unpleasant history that tells tales of myth mixed with reality. Around 1240, Nicholas de Soules built the original castle. By 1318, his descendant William de Soules became Lord of Hermitage but was a deeply unpopular man. William's deep vein of cruelty culminated in stories of him practising the black arts at the castle. Tales of kidnapped children and William desecrating their corpses during satanic rituals reached King Robert the Bruce. In exasperation, Bruce is reported to have cried 'Soules! Soules! Go boil him in brew!' Locals took that at face value and captured William and boiled him alive in molten lead, allegedly, to assuage any supernatural powers he may have had. In fact, in 1320, William contributed to an English plot to assassinate Robert the Bruce. It failed and William was imprisoned in Dumbarton Castle, where he died.

In 1338, the castle was captured by William Douglas, an ambitious man. He took umbrage at King David II's appointment of Alexander Ramsay as Sheriff of Teviotdale. So, he locked Ramsay in the castle and starved him to death. The king then appointed Douglas to the vacant sheriff's job. In 1566, the castle welcomed Mary, Queen of Scots, during her affair with James Hepburn, fourth Earl of Bothwell. Romanticised by Walter Scott in the 1800s, the castle became neglected. Today, ghostlier visitors have been reported, including Redcaps – goblins that plague the Borders, known for soaking their caps in the blood of victims.

Address Newcastleton, Roxburghshire, TD9 0LU (nearest postcode), +44 (0) 1387 376222, www.historicenvironment.scot | Getting there Located off an unnamed road 7 miles east of A 7 (near Fiddleton) and 3 miles west of B 6399 | Hours Daily 1 Apr–30 Sep 10am–4.30pm; not easily accessible by wheelchair users | Tip Hike to Pikethaw Burial Cairn, a rare funerary monument from prehistoric society (Pikethaw Burial Cairn, off the A 7 near Fiddleton, DG13 0HP).

2 Robert the Bruce's Heart

Scottish identity and a 'prune-like' heart

Melrose Abbey was the first Cistercian monastery in Scotland. Founded by King David I in 1136, monastic life at the abbey continued until 1590 when the last monk, John Watson, died. During the Middle Ages, Melrose was on the front line of conflict with England. The abbey required major repairs after attacks by Kings Edward I and II in the early 1300s. King Richard II's attack in 1385 led to a complete rebuilding of the abbey church. And the War of the Rough Wooing in the 1540s caused further damage.

Melrose Abbey was a highly desirable final resting place for the powerful. Privileged people buried there include King Alexander II (d. 1249). But it is the alleged heart of Robert the Bruce (1274–1329), discovered twice at Melrose, that is the star attraction. Referred to as 'Good King Robert', Bruce was the most revered warrior of his generation. He is best known for his alliance with William Wallace and for defeating the English army at Bannockburn in 1314. Romanticised since his death (his body being interred at Dunfermline Abbey), Bruce has become a symbol of Scottish nationhood and identity.

In 1921, an archaeological dig at Melrose Abbey uncovered a medieval cannister holding a 'prune-like' heart. After its reburial, a further excavation in 1996 rediscovered the cannister. Three heart burials at Melrose are recorded. This was a relatively common practice during the medieval period where dissected hearts were submerged in a preservative hot tar, essentially cooking it. The 1996 discovery attributed the heart, probably mistakenly, to Robert the Bruce. It was then reburied again at Melrose. Regardless of whether it is Bruce's heart or not, it played into national political sentiments of the 1990s and Scottish Devolution. Bruce and his rediscovered heart once again became symbolic of Scotland and self-governance – something that Bruce himself fought for.

Address Melrose Abbey, Abbey Street, Melrose, Roxburghshire, TD6 9LG, +44 (0) 1896 822562, www.historicenvironment.scot | **Getting there** Public car park next to abbey; buses 51, 60, 67, 68 and 313 to Abbey Car Park; train to Tweedbank station then a short bus ride or 40-minute walk | **Hours** Daily 1 Apr–30 Sep 9.30am–5pm, 1 Oct–31 Mar 10am–4pm | **Tip** Visit Robert the Bruce's burial place and reconstructed tomb (Dunfermline Abbey and Palace, St Margaret's Street, Dunfermline, Fife, KY12 7PE).

3 *Widows and Bairns*

Heartbroken by Scotland's worst fishing disaster

On 14 October 1881, 189 men and boys perished when their fishing fleet sank during a violent storm. The Great Eyemouth Fishing Disaster, known locally as 'Black Friday', left behind 93 widows, and 267 children (bairns) became fatherless. Scotland had many fishing tragedies during the 19th century, including the 1848 Moray Firth disaster which saw 100 anglers lost on 124 boats. Resultant safety improvements ensued, including decking open-hulled boats, as well as making harbours safer. Anglers in Eyemouth initially resisted the introduction of decked vessels. The harbour at Eyemouth was also not improved, as the town resisted a fishing tithe imposed on them by the Church of Scotland in 1841.

Despite weather warnings, the Eyemouth anglers decided to put to sea because of economic necessity. It was a tradition that if one boat sailed, then all boats in the fleet would sail. After sailing for just three hours about nine miles from shore, the skies darkened, and the wind strengthened to hurricane force. The fleet headed for harbour, but many were swamped while others were smashed on the Hurker Rocks exposed near the harbour entrance. Families ashore saw the carnage, even hearing the screams of loved ones as they drowned, unable to help.

A disaster fund was set up afterwards, with over £50,000 collected (worth over £5 million today). Widows collected five shillings a week unless they remarried and an added two shillings and six pence for each child. Some children were offered places in a Quarrier's Children's Home, but local mothers refused by saying 'we shall keep our bairns for our future of our ports'. As the womenfolk of the town were so tenacious, Eyemouth continued to be a thriving community. Unveiled in 2016 and crafted by Jill Watson, a poignant series of memorials depicts all the 'widows and bairns' looking out to sea in despair.

Address 9 St Ella's Place, Eyemouth, TD14 5HP | Getting there Located near the promenade, *Widows and Bairns* is one of four memorials; others being at nearby St Abbs, Cove and Burnmouth; buses 60, 235 and 253 to Eyemouth Co-Op, then a 5-minute walk | Hours Unrestricted | Tip Visit the Eyemouth Cholera Monument, a watchhouse constructed from tombstones to make room for a burial pit for disease victims (High Street, Eyemouth, TD14 5EY).

4 51st Highlanders

Left behind after the 'Miracle of Dunkirk'

The 51st Highland Division Memorial depicts a young Dutch girl presenting a rose to a kilted piper from the regiment. Commissioned in 1995 to mark the 50th anniversary of peace in Europe, the bronze statue replicates a memorial at Schijndel in the Netherlands. The Division had liberated the town from German occupation on 23 October 1944, with many casualties.

Originally raised in 1908, the 51st Highland Division was a territorial unit made up of part-time volunteer troops. With men mainly drawn from the Highlands, soldiers had to hand in their kilts to the war office, as the traditional outfit was considered unfit to fight in. After initially being known as 'Harper's Duds', for poor performance under the leadership of Major General George Harper, the Highland fighting spirit was recognised at the disastrous Somme offensive in 1916. Though defeated at the battle, Germans referred to the Highlanders as 'The Ladies from Hell'.

In 1940, during the early months of World War II, the Division was part of the British Expeditionary Force (BEF). When the BEF had to make a hasty retreat to the beaches of Dunkirk to escape German forces, the Highlanders stayed behind. As Operation Dynamo liberated the BEF, an evacuation of more than 338,000 troops involving the Royal Navy and a fleet of small boats, the Highlanders bravely fought on. Some suggest that Winston Churchill sacrificed the Division for the survival of the broader BEF. Under the command of General Charles de Gaulle, the Highlanders and the French tried to stop German advances. Despite an evacuation attempt at St Valery, on 12 June the Division surrendered. Over 10,000 men were taken prisoner. They suffered horrendous conditions, though a significant number managed to escape the Stalags. Re-formed, the Division fought in the Mediterranean and Middle East, as well as on D-Day. It was finally disbanded in 1968.

Address 51st Highland Division Memorial, North Inch Park, Perth, PH1 5HG (nearest postcode) | Getting there Located at the southern tip of the park; buses 7, 7A, 57, 57A and 57U to Charlotte Street; train to Perth station then a 15-minute walk | Hours Unrestricted | Tip Visit the King James pub, a former friary where King James I was assassinated in 1437 after trying to hide in a sewer (King James, 73 Kinnoull Street, Perth, PH1 5EZ).

5 Battle of Bannockburn

Scotland's decisive victory against England

From the Battle of Brunanburh in A.D. 937 to the Jacobite Uprisings in the 18th century, the Kingdoms of Scotland and England fought many battles. But the Battle of Bannockburn, fought in 1314 during the First War of Scottish Independence, is a landmark in Scottish history. It cemented Robert the Bruce's grip over Scotland and, arguably, deferred the Union of Scotland and England by almost 300 years.

By 1313, Robert the Bruce had gone from guerrilla leader to self-declared king. Only one English stronghold remained, at Stirling Castle, near the site of an earlier Scottish victory led by William Wallace in 1297. King Edward II of England sent some 18,000 men to relieve the castle, probably the largest English army to invade Scotland. On 23 June 1314, the English vanguard gathered at the ford over Bannock Burn, a few miles south of Stirling. The English at once attacked, but the Scots had laid formidable defences. The main battle took place on 24 June, with the much bigger English army routed by Bruce's relentless attack. Most of the English knights died, and Edward II only just escaped. The battle created the legend of Robert the Bruce, and even today a stoic Scot might raise a smile.

The battle marked the last major victory of the Scots over the English during the Middle Ages. The battle also saw important military tactics where the infantry rather than the cavalry dominated future medieval battlegrounds. The battle was also an attempt by Robert the Bruce to legitimise his kingship through combat. Throughout his life, Bruce had waged war to wear down his Scottish opponents as well as the English regime. He died in 1329. The exact location of the battle is contested, though where the visitor centre is today claims the spot. Visitors can follow in the footsteps of Robert the Bruce and digitally immerse themselves in battle scenes 'slippery with blood and piled with the dead'.

Address Battle of Bannockburn Visitor Centre, Glasgow Road, Whins of Milton, Stirling, FK7 0LJ, +44 (0) 1786 812664, www.nts.org.uk/visit/places/bannockburn | Getting there M80/M9 (Junction 9) and follow A 872 towards Stirling – the centre is about 2 miles from the motorway, on the west side of the A 872 | Hours Visitor Centre & Battle Experience, daily 3 Jan – 21 Dec 10am – 5pm; tickets for Battle Experience must be pre-booked | Tip Hidden in a modern shopping centre is the Bastion and Thieves' Pot, a relic of 16th-century capital punishment (Port Street entrance, 17 – 21 Thistle Centre, Stirling, FY8 2DL).

6__Battle of Killiecrankie

One of the goriest clashes in Jacobite history

Killiecrankie Pass is a steep-sided valley cut by the River Garry. It is a splendid trail offering a striking chunk of Scottish scenery. Linking the Lowlands with the Highlands, the route is a Site of Special Scientific Interest. In 1884, Queen Victoria visited the Pass and wrote, 'I cannot describe how beautiful it is. Albert was in perfect ecstasies'.

But the Pass has a gory past. On 27 July 1689, against the 'Glorious Revolution', 4,000 English troops gathered for the Battle of Killiecrankie. Led by General Hugh Mackay, the English were met by brutal Jacobite resistance under the command of John Graham, First Viscount of Dundee. As the English approached the northern end of the Pass, a cavalry officer was killed by a Jacobite sniper. Today, the spot is where the railway viaduct stands and is known as Trooper's Den. With the smaller Jacobite army occupying the higher points of the glen, English troops took up positions on lower slopes, with their backs to the river. As English cannon fire proved ineffective shooting uphill, the Viscount's men waited until sundown and then charged downhill. Carnage ensued and over 2,000 of Mackay's soldiers were slain. However, one lucky redcoat called Donald McBane escaped by jumping 18 feet across the gorge, known today as Soldier's Leap.

The Jacobites won the day, but Viscount Dundee was mortally wounded by a musket ball. Without Dundee in charge, the 1689 Jacobite Uprising rapidly failed, and it was the first in a series of conflicts that would lead to the ultimate Jacobite demise at the Battle of Culloden in 1746. Today, this bloody episode adds a supernatural twist to the natural beauty of the Pass. Stories abound of carriages in the 1800s and cars in the 1900s being pursued by ghostly forms; a blood-red glow appearing over the battlefield; and visitors seeing the dead lying where they fell, over three centuries ago.

Address Killiecrankie Visitor Centre, Killiecrankie, near Pitlochry, Perthshire, PH16 5LG, +44 (0) 1796 473233, www.nts.org.uk/visit/places/killiecrankie | **Getting there** National Cycle Route 7, follow B 8079 (from the A 924), 3 miles north of Pitlochry; steep and uneven paths with steps throughout the Pass | **Hours** Visitor Centre daily 10am–4pm, closed Christmas and New Year; site and paths unrestricted year round | **Tip** Visit the ancient Birnam Wood, immortalised in Shakespeare's tragic play of murder and revenge, *Macbeth* (Oak Road, Dunkeld, Birnam, PH8 0BL).

7 Battle of the Clans

Most bizarre fight in Scottish clan history

During medieval times, every neighbouring clan in the Highlands appears to have fought each other. Yet, the Battle of the North Inch – or 'Battle of the Clans' – during September 1396 in Perth is probably the most bizarre. While details have been lost to myth, the Battle of the Clans was a stage-managed fight between two feuding clans, the Chattan Confederation and the 'Clan Kay'.

Earlier feuds between the clans had resulted in the Battle of Invernahavon (1370 or 1386). Epidemic feuding put Lowland nobles in fear of an even greater conflict. So, at the behest of King Robert III to settle grievances, a mass duel was organised in what is now North Inch Park, Perth. The winners would claim victory and the losers would be offered a pardon. The 'Inch' (meaning 'island') was, and is still, a flat and grassy meadow. It was the ideal place for the battle, as the king was staying at a local monastery, and Perth was seen as the last bastion of civilisation before the Highlands. In an early form of 'dark tourism', the Royal Court and many of the local populace travelled to see the spectacle.

Essentially a trial by combat, 30 men from each clan assembled for a supervised fight to the death. Each combatant was allowed three arrows, a shield (known as a *targe*), a *dirk* (knife), and a weapon of choice (either a sword or battleaxe). In his 1828 book *The Fair Maid of Perth*, novelist Sir Walter Scott describes the battle scene as '...blood flowed fast, and the groans of those who fell began to mingle with those who fought... dead or dying; arms and legs lopped off, heads cleft to the chin, slashes deep through the shoulder to the breast, showed at once the fury of the combat'.

The Chattans killed all but one of their opponents at the cost of 19 deaths of their own. The last remaining survivor of Clan Kay, realising his fate, jumped into the River Tay and was never seen again.

Address North Inch Park, Perth, PH1 5HG | Getting there A 5-minute walk from the city centre; a stone plinth on the North Inch opposite the Blackfriars plaque commemorates the Battle of the Clans; Pay & Display car parking available at Bell's Sport Centre (PH1 5HS) | Hours Unrestricted | Tip Visit nearby Scone Palace, the crowning place of Scottish kings and the tumultuous history of the Stone of Destiny, a symbol of Scottish nationhood (Scone Palace, Perth, PH2 6BD, www.scone-palace.co.uk).

8 The Black Watch

The oldest Highland army regiment

After the First Jacobite Rebellion of 1715, the need to 'police' the Highlands became paramount for the British crown. Companies of militia were raised from loyalist clans to 'watch' over the Highlands. These companies, known in Gaelic as *Am Freiceadan Dubh* or 'The Black Watch', were unpopular for their policing role and dark green (almost black) government-issued tartan kilts. In 1739, King George II ordered more companies be raised into a single infantry regiment. In 1795, the Red Hackle was adopted as a distinctive feature of the regiment's uniform. Since then, The Black Watch have played significant roles in the bloody conflicts that have shaped the modern world.

With impressive Highland fighting tenacity, the regiment first fought at Fontenoy (War of the Austrian Succession) in 1745. During the American War of Independence (1775–83), the Watch defeated George Washington at the Battle of Long Island. It served during the Frontier Wars (1779–1878), as well as the Napoleonic Wars (1803–15). The Watch was mentioned in dispatches at the Battle of Waterloo (1815). During the Victorian era, the Watch fought in the Crimean War (1854–56), the Indian Mutiny (1857–59), and the Boer War (1899–1902). During World War I, the regiment lost over 8,000 men, while it served in most major theatres of World War II. In the post-war period, the Watch has served in Korea (1950–53), the Mau Mau Revolt in Kenya (1952–60), Northern Ireland (1969–2007) and Iraq (2003–11), and it was the final garrison to leave Hong Kong during its handover to China in 1997.

The museum of The Black Watch charts the illustrious past of the regiment and brings its history to life. It is housed within Balhousie Castle in Perth, which dates from the 12th century. Remodelled in the 1860s in the Scottish Baronial style, the castle became the Regimental HQ and museum of The Black Watch in 2009.

Address The Black Watch Museum, Balhousie Castle, Hay Street, Perth, PH1 5HR, +44 (0) 1738 638152, www.theblackwatch.co.uk | Getting there Train to Perth station then a 15-minute walk; buses 1A, 9 and 615 to Balhousie Avenue then a 5-minute walk | Hours Daily 1 Nov–31 Mar 10am–4pm, 1 Apr–31 Oct 9.30am–4.30pm | Tip Visit the Earthquake House, which lies on the Highland Boundary Fault that suffers the most tremors in the UK and is the first dedicated earthquake observatory in the world (Earthquake House, Comrie, Crieff, Perthshire, PH6 2JU).

9 Bon Scott Statue

Tribute to a tragic rock star

Bagpipes under one arm and holding a microphone aloft, a statue of a rock icon stands in Kirriemuir. Ronald Belford 'Bon' Scott, born on 9 July 1946 in Forfar, lived in Kirriemuir until he was six years old. In 1952, Scott's family emigrated to Australia, settling in Fremantle. Scott pursued his love of music by joining a local Scots pipe band at school. It was here that he earned the nickname 'Bonny' Scott, which he later shortened to 'Bon'. He went on to become the lead vocalist of the Australian band AC/DC.

Scott formed his first band The Spektors in 1964 and sang with The Valentines and Fraternity. In 1974, he replaced Dave Evans as lead singer of AC/DC and had commercial success and critical acclaim. AC/DC were formed in 1973 in Sydney as a hard-rock band by Glasgow-born brothers Malcom and Angus Young. The band have been cited as a formative influence on the emergence of heavy metal music. As an abbreviation for 'alternating current/direct current' electricity, the name of AC/DC symbolised the band's raw energy and the power-driven performances of their music. Scott performed on the band's first seven albums, with *Highway to Hell* in 1979 as their commercial breakthrough.

Tragically, Scott's renowned heavy-drinking habits caused his death on 19 February 1980. He was 33 years old. After partying the night before in London, a very drunk Scott was fatefully left on the back seat of a car 'to sleep it off'. The coroner concluded he died of acute alcohol poisoning and recorded 'death by misadventure'. Today, Kirriemuir annually hosts 'BonFest', a tribute music festival to Bon Scott. Unveiled in 2016 and sculpted by John McKenna, Scott's statute is a rock music pilgrimage destination. In Palmyra, Australia, where Scott is buried, his grave has become a cultural landmark and a classified heritage place. It is reportedly the most visited grave in Australia.

Address Bellies Brae, Kirriemuir, Angus, DD8 4EB, www.visitangus.com/bon-scott-statue | Getting there Scott's statue is in Bellies Brae car park; buses 20, 27 and 128 to Bank Street then a 5-minute walk | Hours Unrestricted | Tip Visit the Scott-Wilson Memorial, commemorating Captain Scott and Dr Wilson's ill-fated expedition to the South Pole in 1912, planned at Wilson's home in Glen Prosen (on the approach road to Glen Prosen, Angus, DD8 4ND).

10 Cultybraggan PoW Camp

'Black Camp of the North'

Nestled below the rugged Aberuchill Hills near the picturesque village of Comrie is the UK's best-preserved prisoner of war (PoW) camp. It is also Scotland's last remaining PoW camp of World War II. Built in 1941 and known as 'Camp 21' or the 'Black Camp of the North', Cultybraggan was one of two high-security PoW camps in Britain. With over 80 Nissen huts, it was initially used as a labour camp for Italian PoWs. Later, the 4,500-prisoner capacity camp became a place of internment for German Nazis.

German PoWs categorised as 'black' were considered the most ardent Nazis. Prisoners categorised as 'white' or 'grey' had lesser Nazi sympathies and were allowed to work in local communities. In 2014, former Waffen-SS member Heinrich Steinmeyer left £384,000 in his will to elderly residents of Comrie for the 'kindness and generosity' he had received while imprisoned at Cultybraggan. However, Cultybraggan gained notoriety after the murder of PoW Wolfgang Rosterg. Known for his anti-Nazi views, and mistakenly categorised as 'black', other Nazi PoWs tried him in a kangaroo court. Rosterg was beaten with heated rods and then lynched. Six PoWs were court-martialled: one was given a life sentence and five were hanged at Pentonville Prison, London – the last ever mass-execution in Britain.

The final PoWs left in 1947, and in 1948 Cultybraggan became a military training camp. In 1960, during the Cold War, a subterranean Regional Government HQ bunker was built. Completed in 1990 at a cost of £30 million, the bunker was constructed over two floors. It would have been used as a command-and-control hub in case of a nuclear war. The bunker closed in 1992 and is now used for data storage for an IT company. Today, the camp is a multi-use community resource and includes a small museum. Cultybraggan is named by Historic Scotland as a Unique Heritage Asset of International Value.

Address Cultybraggan Camp Museum, Hut 3, Cultybraggan Camp, Comrie, Perthshire, PH6 2AB, +44 (0) 1764 670769, www.cultybraggancamp.uk | Getting there Situated a mile south of Comrie, off B 827; train to Dunblane station (but the Camp is 19 miles from there); buses to Comrie | Hours Museum Apr–Oct 10.30am–4.30pm; campgrounds unrestricted all year | Tip Visit Lady Kentmores Antiques, a haunting collection of items that are the stuff of nightmares (35 Mains Street, Callander, FK17 8DX).

11 Curse of Patrick Hamilton

Malediction for University of St Andrews students

The University of St Andrews was founded in 1413 by a group of Augustinian clergies driven from the University of Paris by the Papal Schism (a Catholic church crisis during 1378–1417). After being granted a series of papal bulls (decrees from the Pope), St Andrews was encouraged to teach Catholic doctrine. However, with the Scottish Reformation, a 16th-century process where Scotland shunned Catholicism, the university became a Protestant institution in 1560.

Father Patrick Hamilton, a former student of St Andrews, was an early Scottish Protestant Reformer. The reforming doctrines of Martin Luther, a German theologian who introduced Lutheranism, captivated Hamilton. Eager to communicate them to his compatriots, Hamilton came to the attention of the Archbishop of St Andrews, James Beaton, who issued an arrest warrant for his 'heretical preaching'. Hamilton fled to Germany in 1527 only to be invited back to St Andrews by Cardinal David Beaton, the nephew of James Beaton. Hamilton was allowed to preach and debate, even publishing his 'Patrick's Places', which introduced Luther's Law and Gospel into Scottish theology.

However, Hamilton was soon summoned before a council presided over by Cardinal Beaton, and charged with heretical teachings. Found guilty, Hamilton was ordered to be burned at the stake. Outside St Salvator's College and Chapel, the execution fire raged for six hours, during which 24-year-old Hamilton reportedly unleashed a curse for all future students of St Andrews to be burned to death. Today, the initials PH are set into cobbles at the execution spot to commemorate Hamilton's martyrdom. University myth calls for students to avoid stepping on the monogram for fear of being cursed. In 2005, HRH Prince William and his future wife, Catherine Middleton, future monarchs of the United Kingdom, both graduated from the University of St Andrews.

Address 75 North Street, St Andrews, Fife, KY16 9AL – located on the pavement outside St Salvator's Chapel | **Getting there** Buses 92, 94 and 94A; train to Leuchars station, then shuttle bus to St Andrews | **Hours** Unrestricted | **Tip** Visit the George Wishart Memorial Stones, where initials GW mark where another Protestant martyr was burned at the stake by Cardinal Beaton (St Andrews Castle, The Scores, St Andrews, KY16 9AR, www.historicenvironment.scot/visit-a-place/places/st-andrews-castle).

12 David Stirling Memorial

The 'Phantom Major' of the SAS

Gazing towards the Trossachs hills is a statue of Colonel Sir David Stirling (1915–1990), a pioneer of the United Kingdom Special Forces. Born into an aristocratic Scottish family near Doune, Stirling was a wayward character but a natural leader. An inveterate gambler with a fondness for nightlife, he baulked at the conventional way of life. Thrown out of Cambridge University, Stirling was a keen mountaineer and a Scots Guard.

When World War II broke out in 1939, Stirling, who had been working as a cowboy in the USA, returned to the UK and joined the elite Commandoes. However, frustrated with cancelled operations of the Commandoes, Stirling decided to create an army unit of his own in North Africa. Using his social connections, Stirling drew in adventure-hungry recruits from the Commandoes. With just 67 men, his unit was called 'L Detachment Special Air Service', part of an intelligence bluff to exaggerate its small numbers. With a motto of 'Who Dares Wins', and with the support of Churchill and overcoming military bureaucracy, the new SAS caused mayhem behind enemy lines. Although the first mission – Operation Squatter – was a disaster, the SAS destroyed hundreds of enemy planes in daring covert raids. The Germans nicknamed Stirling 'The Phantom Major'. Field Marshall Montgomery said, 'The boy Stirling is quite mad, quite, quite mad. However, in a war there is often a place for mad people'.

Stirling was captured but escaped four times before being sent to Colditz in Germany. The SAS continued to wreak havoc for the enemy under the command of Colonel Robert 'Paddy' Mayne. After the war, Stirling went on to create controversial private military companies, including serving as a mercenary and arms dealer. He even planned initial attempts to take over the British government during the 1970s. The SAS remain an elite special forces regiment of the British army.

Address The David Stirling Memorial (or SAS Memorial) near Dunblane, Kier, Stirlingshire, FK15 9NY (nearest postcode) | Getting there 2 miles south-east of Doune, off the B 824 – car park near the memorial; train to Dunblane station then a 20-minute walk | Hours Unrestricted | Tip Hike to the Meikle Bin Plane Crash Site and see wreckage of a military plane that crashed in the Campsie Fells in 1950 (Meikle Bin, near the summit, Carron Valley, Todholes, G63 0XL).

13 Dunblane Memorial

Most murderous mass shooting in British history

The devil visited Dunblane on 13 March 1996. At 9.30am, 43-year-old Thomas Hamilton invaded Dunblane Primary School and killed 16 children and their 45-year-old teacher, Gwen Mayor. In the school gym, carrying four handguns and 743 rounds of ammunition and wearing shooting earmuffs, Hamilton fired into a group of five- and six-year-old children as they were preparing for PE. He continued his fusillade by firing at random, before shooting point-blank range at children incapacitated by earlier shots. Hamilton then committed suicide. In less than four minutes, 32 adults and children had sustained gunshot wounds. Among the children attending the school during the attack were Andy Murray (aged 8) and his brother Jamie (aged 10), of British tennis fame.

The tragedy imprinted the UK's cultural consciousness. Hamilton was a former Scout leader who ran clubs for boys. Andy Murray is said to have attended one of the boys' clubs as a child. But Hamilton was dogged by rumours of inappropriate behaviour towards young boys. Suspicious of his moral intentions, the Scouts Association blacklisted him. While some parents made formal complaints, no legal action was ever taken against Hamilton. Instead, he viewed himself as a victim of a sinister witch-hunt. Though a definitive motive for the attack was never outlined, Hamilton had referenced Dunblane Primary School in a letter looking to clear his name.

In the aftermath of the slaughter, Dunblane residents started the Snowdrop Campaign calling for change in gun-ownership laws. Following the official inquiry and Cullen Report, the UK government enacted tough new gun-ownership laws across Great Britain. Apart from a mass shooting in 2010 in Cumbria, England, Dunblane is Britain's last but deadliest mass shooting. In 1998, a memorial garden was opened at Dunblane Cemetery where Gwen Mayor and 12 of her murdered pupils are buried.

Address Dunblane Cemetery, 8 Bellenden Grove, Dunblane, FK15 0FD | Getting there The Dunblane Memorial Garden is found at the rear of the cemetery; buses 15A, 20, 148, 326 and 925 to Kippendavie Road | Hours Daily 8am – 8pm | Tip Visit the Sheriffmuir Atlantic Wall, a 1943 mock site to rehearse for the D-Day landings and practise against Nazi coastal fortifications (Stirling Road, Dunblane, FK15 0LN, www.atlanticwalls.uk).

14 Forbes Mausoleum

An abandoned monument to mortality

Fused with elements of Scottish Baronial architecture, Callendar House is a 14th-century mansion in the style of a French Renaissance château. During its 600-year history, the house has welcomed many illustrious guests, including Mary, Queen of Scots, Oliver Cromwell, Bonnie Prince Charlie and Queen Victoria. The house is built on the line of the Antonine Wall, a Roman turf fortification that crossed the Central Belt of Scotland in A.D. 142. In 1345, the Callendar lands were granted to Sir William Livingston by King David II, son of Robert the Bruce. In 1783, the estate was sold to William Forbes after the Earl of Linlithgow lost it following the 1715 Jacobite Uprising.

Forbes was a prosperous Aberdeen-based coppersmith, and the greatest landowner in Scotland at the time. He produced a £100,000 banknote which he had specially printed for the purchase of the Callendar estate. With connections to the slave trade in the Caribbean, Forbes was unpopular with local people, though his family kept great influence over the area for two centuries. Wishing to be a 'landed gentleman', Forbes made expensive alterations to the house, while keeping servant quarters as cheap as possible. Forbes was eventually included in Burke's *Landed Gentry*, a definitive list of families in possession of landed property.

Deep inside the grounds of Callendar House lies an abandoned mausoleum. Dating from 1816, the circular classical monument is the interment site of nine members of the Forbes family, including William Dudley Forbes who died in 1977. Servants of the estate were buried nearby, but their gravestones have been smashed. The mausoleum is now tattooed with graffiti and the door sealed. Above the entrance, a Greek inscription from a verse by the poet Lucian translates as 'Mortals; possessions are mortal, and all things pass us by; if not, at any rate we pass them by'.

Address Callendar House & Park, Falkirk, FK1 1YR, +44 (0) 1324 503772, www.falkirkleisureandculture.org/venues/callendar-house | Getting there Buses 1, F16, F25 and X38; train to Falkirk High and Falkirk Grahamston stations; free car parking via Seaton Place | Hours Mon, Wed–Sun 10am–5pm, closed Tue and Sun mid Oct–mid Apr | Tip Visit the Lilias Adie Grave Marker, the final resting place of an accused witch (Main Street, Torryburn, KY12 8LT).

15 Martyrs' Memorial

Sisters of 'The Killing Time'

A haunting monument stands prominently in Stirling's Old Town Cemetery. The iconic Martyrs' Memorial, with an angel overlooking two sisters reading the Bible, commemorates 'The Killing Time'. From 1679 to the Glorious Revolution of 1688, conflict between Presbyterian Covenanters and Kings Charles II and James VI saw thousands of people killed for their religious beliefs. Important in the martyrology of the Church of Scotland, The Killing Time saw increasing state control over spiritual matters. Covenanters declared King Charles II the 'anti-Christ' at the Sanquhar Declaration in 1680 and renounced all allegiance to the Crown. This was treason.

Those caught worshipping their Presbyterian faith in covert conventicles (often in fields or houses) were tortured or executed for sedition. In 1685, at Wigton in Dumfries and Galloway, two sisters – Margaret (18) and Agnes (14) Wilson – together with 63-year-old Margaret MacLaughlin were charged with attending conventicles. The Wilsons were daughters of Gilbert Wilson – an Episcopalian – meaning he had embraced the king's reforms. Yet Margaret and Agnes remained devout Covenanters. The three women were sentenced to death on 13 April 1685, though Agnes' sentence was commuted after Gilbert paid a £100 bond. The two Margarets were tied to a stake on 11 May 1685 in the Solway Firth below the high-water mark. Watched over by family who prayed and sang hymns, including Gilbert, the condemned refused to recant. As the incoming tide rose, the women drowned. They were buried in the churchyard in Wigton.

William Drummond, a fervent Presbyterian, funded the Martyrs' Memorial depicting Margaret and Agnes Wilson so the sad episode would be forever remembered. Erected in 1859, a protective cupola was added in 1867. Some say the addition of the glass canopy stops the spirits of the sisters escaping and seeking revenge.

Address Old Town Cemetery, The Back Walk, Stirling, FK8 1EG, www.oldtowncemetery.co.uk | **Getting there** Train to Stirling station then a 15-minute walk; bus P2 to Youth Hostel or Bow Street | **Hours** Unrestricted | **Tip** Visit Stirling Old Town Jail to have immersive experiences of historic punishment with bloody tales of victims and villains (Old Town Jail, St John Street, Stirling, FY8 1EA, www.oldtownjail.co.uk).

16 National Wallace Monument

From outlaw to 'Braveheart'

Sir William Wallace is one of the most evocative figures from Scottish history. Born during the 1270s, Wallace became an outlaw, killing a son of an English castle constable as well as two English soldiers. 'The Wallace' was never a king, but his name as a 'freedom fighter' lives on. His notable deeds were opposing King Edward I of England from gaining supremacy over Scotland in around 1300.

Scotland was ruled as a province of England in 1297. When the Sheriff of Lanark, Sir William Heselrig, executed Marion Braidfoot – the apparent secret bride of Wallace – Wallace killed Heselrig, massacred every English solider and besieged Dundee Castle. Fearing an uprising, King Edward I sent troops to secure the fortress at Stirling Castle. On 11 September 1297, Wallace routed the English at the Battle of Stirling Bridge. However, on 22 July 1298, the English returned to victory at the Battle of Falkirk. Wallace resigned the guardianship of Scotland in favour of Robert the Bruce and John Comyn III. Returning from France, Wallace was betrayed and imprisoned at Dumbarton Castle. Wallace arrived for trial at Westminster Hall in London on 23 August 1305. Found guilty of treason, he was hanged until almost dead. Revived, he had his intestines 'drawn' from his body. His body was quartered and displayed in Newcastle, Berwick, Stirling and Perth. His tarred head was placed on a spike on London Bridge.

Romanticised throughout history, including in a 1477 poem by the bard Blind Harry, and later by Sir Walter Scott in the 1800s, Wallace became a source of Scottish national identity. In 1995, the movie *Braveheart* starring Mel Gibson brought Wallace another layer of artistic licence. Despite debates over Wallace and his military importance, a national monument was completed in 1869. Today, the myth of Wallace endures and is still hugely influential in Scottish nationalism.

Address Abbey Craig, Hillfoots Road, Causewayhead, Stirling, FK9 5LF, +44 (0) 1786 472140, www.nationalwallacemonument.com | Getting there Buses 52 and UL (Unilink) every 30 minutes; free car parking | Hours See website for seasonal hours | Tip Visit the 'Beheading Stone' and its axe marks, once a chopping block for public medieval executions (Mote Hill, Back O' Hill Road, Stirling, FK8 1AA).

17 Scotland's Secret Bunker

'Protect and survive' a nuclear Armageddon

The 'Secret' Bunker is probably the worst 'best-kept' secret in Scotland. Yet from 1951 when the bunker was built, until it was decommissioned in 1993, this was Scotland's secret place. Opened in 1994 as a visitor attraction and museum, the bunker had been Scotland's Underground Nuclear Command Centre. Located near St Andrews, the bunker would have been the twilight world of Scottish government in case of nuclear war.

Concealed by an innocent-looking farmhouse and domestic dwelling, the bunker is buried from view. At 100 feet underground and spread across a labyrinth of two levels, the bunker is encased in 15 feet of reinforced concrete. Its original purpose in the 1950s was as an RAF radar station. As part of the British ROTOR system, it offered air defence to counter possible attack by Soviet bombers. It was later developed as a command centre in the face of nuclear annihilation during the Cold War. Accommodating up to 300 personnel, the bunker has two cinemas, a café, the nuclear operations room, an RAF control centre, a BBC studio, a chapel and dormitories. While millions of people would have lain dead and dying across Scotland if nuclear war had come, a vain attempt to carry on would have been made in the bunker.

The Cold War was an illusory war full of 'barren battlefields' that never 'heated up'. As a political stand-off between the West (led by the USA) and the East (led by the former USSR), the Cold War lasted from 1945 until the break-up of the Soviet Union in the late 1980s/early 1990s. The period saw important architectural and technological progress, including the Secret Bunker. To 'protect and survive' nuclear Armageddon, the bunker is a visible reminder that we live in a post-Cold War cultural environment. Yet, today, the threat of nuclear conflict is still real, and there may be other secret bunkers out there – or yet to be built.

Address Troywood, Fife, KY16 8QH, +44 (0) 1333 310301, www.secretbunker.co.uk | **Getting there** Off the B 940, 3.5 miles north-west of Crail; car parking available; multiple stairs with no lift access available | **Hours** Daily 1 Feb–2 Nov 10am–5pm | **Tip** Visit the Covenanter's Grave where severed body parts of three men were buried after being executed during the 17th-century Killing Times (Cupar Cemetery, Ashlar Lane, Cupar, KY15 5AL).

18 The Star Pyramid

Remembering religious and civil persecution

At the foot of Stirling Castle stands a huge sandstone ashlar pyramid. Known as Salem Rock, the unusual memorial is dedicated to all those who suffered martyrdom for civil and religious liberty in Scotland. While not commemorating anyone specific, the Star Pyramid recognises the social turbulence and violent strife often caused by differences in religious beliefs and civil frameworks. Notably, England as the dominant country in Great Britain, had long persecuted the Scots. With Scotland adopting predominantly Calvinist doctrines and Presbyterian structures, it was at odds with England. Religious disputes were as much about political principles, due to the assumption that 'true religion and true government' were one and the same.

Over centuries, tens of thousands of Scots have died because of persecution. So, in 1863, William Drummond (1760–1824) – a land surveyor and nurseryman from Stirling – decided to commemorate Scotland's religious and civil struggles. Overlooking the Old Town Cemetery, Drummond laid out the 'Drummond Pleasure Garden'. The cemetery grounds were once used for jousting, as well as an execution site. In his pleasure garden, Drummond commissioned a pyramid from William Barclay, complete with marble Bibles and biblical quotations. A Bible and Confession of Faith are sealed within an inner chamber.

Twice married, with 15 children, Drummond and his family founded an agricultural museum in the 1830s. They pioneered turnip development with the Drummond's 'Improved Swede' and 'Extra Improved Swede'. Drummond was also a devout evangelist and obsessed with religion. With his brother Peter, they published religious tracts through the Drummond Tract Enterprise for preachers, missionaries and Sunday schools. By 1872, 60 million tracts had been published. The company closed in 1980. Drummond's sarcophagus lies within a few feet of the Star Pyramid.

Address Valley Lane, Cemetery Road, Stirling, FY8 1EG | Getting there Bus P2 to Bow Street; train to Stirling station then a 15-minute walk | Hours Unrestricted | Tip Visit the Boer War Memorial, commemorating 149 men from the Argyle and Sutherland Highlanders who died in the South African conflict, between 1899 and 1902 (Castle Esplanade, Stirling Castle, Stirling, FY8 1EJ).

19 The Tay Bridge Disaster

Poor engineering leads to 'touching deaths'

By the 1860s, rivalry between Scottish railway companies had taken hold. Controlling key rail routes through Scotland depended on which company would be first to bridge the River Tay at Dundee. Costing £300,000 (£44 million today) and the longest bridge in the world at the time, the (first) Tay Rail Bridge opened in 1877. Engineer Thomas Bouch designed the bridge – 20 men were killed during its construction. Bouch's plans were criticised from the start and had to be revised on grounds of stability. Queen Victoria crossed the bridge in the summer of 1879.

During a violent storm on 28 December 1879, 13 high girders of the central bridge gave way. The bridge collapsed into the River Tay and took with it a North British Railway train travelling from Edinburgh to Aberdeen. All 59 people on board perished with only 46 bodies recovered. Some believe more people were aboard the train. One of the victims was 37-year-old David Neish, a schoolteacher who lived at 51 Coupar Street, Dundee. Three weeks after David's body was recovered, the corpse of a young girl washed up on Wormit Beach. Identified as five-year-old Bella Neish, she was the daughter of David – and had travelled with her father against her mother's wishes. A penny and gold brooch were found in her pocket. Her death certificate says her demise was 'a touching death'.

A Court of Inquiry blamed the bridge design for the collapse, including a failure to consider wind loading. Its judgement rested on Thomas Bouch. The incident was the second deadliest rail disaster in Scotland, surpassed by the 1915 Quintinshill signal-fault accident where 227 people died. Two memorial sites, unveiled in 2013, on both sides of the River Tay in Dundee and Fife commemorate the 1879 tragedy. Parallel to the fallen bridge, a second Tay Rail Bridge opened in 1887. It was built near to the first bridge stumps, which still stand today.

Address Tay Bridge Memorials (north side), Riverside Drive (A 85), Dundee, DD1 4DB/ (south side) Tay Street, Newport-on-Tay, DD6 8AG | Getting there Buses 77B, 92, MD1, MD2 and MD6; north side – train to Dundee station then a 30-minute-walk; ample car parking | Hours Unrestricted | Tip Visit the Grissel Jaffray Memorial, a pavement mosaic marking the execution spot of the last accused witch in Dundee, in 1669 (junction of Peter Street & 61–63 Murraygate, Dundee, DD1 2EA).

20 The 'Witch' Monument

Murdered by the state for 'diabolic pacts'

Between the early 16th and mid-18th centuries, witchcraft was prevalent in Scotland. Up to 4,000 people, mostly from the Scottish Lowlands, were tried for diabolic pacts with the devil – a much higher rate than neighbouring England. Over 1,500 people were executed for being a 'witch', with 70 per cent of them women. Murdered by the state, most were tortured, strangled and then burned.

Today, witchcraft is denounced as pseudo-religious persecution. However, early commemoration of victims was rare, so a unique monument to a specific witch in the Perthshire countryside is a mystery. At 20 feet tall and resembling a cairn with a large stone cross, the monument at Dunning bears the inscription 'Maggie Wall burnt here 1657 as a witch'. It is the only memorial in Scotland of its kind, and is believed to have been erected in the 1790s. Yet, despite the imposing structure, there is no historical evidence that Maggie Wall was a witch – or that she even existed. In nearby Kincladie Wood, records show three witches and a wizard being executed. In 1662, Dunning had its own witchcraft trials, but there is no mention of Maggie. Even the claim that Maggie's skull now rests at Glasgow's Saracen Head pub is disputed.

An 1829 OS map shows that a forest once stood where the monument now stands. It was called 'Maggie Walls Wood' or 'Muggie Walls Wood'. One theory is that the landowner constructed the monument as a composite for all victims of witchcraft. And putting a symbolic Christian cross on the monument for a heretic perhaps illustrates disaffection against the Church. Whatever the causes for witchery, whether economic distress, rise of the 'godly state', or the inquisitorial Scottish judicial system, many victims fell foul of the politics of the day. Maggie may not have existed, but the 'memory' of many other real victims is bound up in the spirit of this haunting memorial.

Address Off the B8062, Auchterarder Road, Dunning, Perth and Kinross, PH2 0QS (nearest postcode) | **Getting there** The monument is 1 mile west of Dunning; no car parking but places to stop with care | **Hours** Unrestricted | **Tip** See the Sir Jimmy Shand Statue, a larger-than-life tribute to the celebrated accordion player (Newburgh Road, Auchtermuchty, Cupar, Fife, KY14 7BS).

21 Devil's Porridge Museum

'Canary Girls' who produced war munitions

World War I was a conflict caused by alliances, imperialism, militarism and nationalism. Over two million German soldiers died, with many of them killed by British artillery shells. To make the shells, the village of Gretna – famous for romantic elopements – became the site of the world's largest cordite factory. HM Factory Gretna made 'Devil's Porridge', a mixture of gun cotton and nitro-glycerine that produced cordite as a shell propellant.

After *The Times* newspaper reported a lack of ammunition for British forces in May 1915, the 'Shell Crisis' became a government priority. David Lloyd George, who was Minister of Munitions, embarked upon constructing HM Factory Gretna. A sprawling assembly of hastily erected wooden huts and brick-built manufacturing sheds, the factory stretched over two miles wide and nine miles in length across the English border. From Dornock in Dumfries & Galloway to Longtown in Cumbria, HM Factory Gretna was supplied by 125 miles of narrow-gauge railway and served by a fireless locomotive. Built in late 1915, the factory recruited chemists, explosives experts and engineers from across the (then) British Empire to organise and manage cordite production.

Two townships were built, complete with schools, cinema, dance halls and a hospital, to accommodate 30,000 factory workers – including 12,000 women. It was predominately young women who mixed the highly volatile 'Devil's Porridge' paste through to producing the finished cordite propellant. Sir Arthur Conan Doyle, creator of Sherlock Holmes, coined the phrase 'Devil's Porridge', after visiting the factory as a war correspondent and seeing the women mix the dangerous concoction. These women were exposed to toxic chemicals in the 'Porridge', which saw their skin turn yellow, and were nicknamed 'Canary Girls'. Other ailments suffered included toxic jaundice, nausea and respiratory disorders.

Address Stanfield, Annan Road, Eastriggs, Dumfries & Galloway, DG12 6TF, +44 (0) 1461 700021, www.devilsporridge.org.uk | Getting there Located on B 721 between Annan and Gretna; bus 79 from Carlisle/Annan; train to Gretna Green station then a lengthy walk; national Cycle Route 7 | Hours Mon–Sat 10am–5pm, Sun 10am–4pm | Tip See the Quintinshill Railway Accident Plaque, commemorating Britain's worst railway disaster in 1915 where 227 people died, including 215 soldiers heading for Gallipoli (Blacksmith's Visitor Centre car park, Gretna Green, Dumfries & Galloway, DG16 5EB).

22 Lockerbie Memorial Garden

Deadliest ever terrorist attack in the UK

On 21 December 1988, Pan Am Flight 103 was flying over Lockerbie on a transatlantic flight from Frankfurt to Detroit. Known as *Clipper Maid of the Seas*, the Boeing 747 exploded from a terrorist bomb hidden in the luggage compartment. All 243 passengers and 16 crew were killed. A further 11 residents of Sherwood Crescent and Rosebank Crescent in Lockerbie died when the plane crashed to earth leaving a crater 154 feet long. The British Geological Survey registered a seismic event at 7.03pm attributed to the impact.

The Libyan regime under Colonel Gaddafi was suspected of the Lockerbie Bombing. While others have been accused, including the Iranian government, various Palestinian terrorist organisations and even Mossad (the Israeli intelligence service), Gaddafi took responsibility and paid compensation to victims' families in 2003. In 2001, Abdelbaset al-Megrahi, who was Head of Security for Libyan Arab Airlines and believed to be a Libyan intelligence officer, was found guilty in a Scottish court (based in The Netherlands) of 270 counts of murder. In 2009, he was released from prison on compassionate grounds and died of cancer in 2012, aged 60. Debates remain to suggest Megrahi was not responsible for the atrocity.

Some passengers remained alive after impact but died soon afterwards. Thirty-five victims were students from Syracuse University, New York. Other prominent victims were Bernt Carlsson, the UN Commissioner for Namibia (then Southwest Africa); James Fuller, CEO of Volkswagen USA; Peter Dix, an Irish Olympic sailor; and English rock musician Paul Jeffreys. Victims hailed from 21 countries and ranged from 2 months to 82 years old, with 41 per cent being 25 years or younger. Many of the bodies strewed the local landscape while some were never recovered.

Address Dryfesdale Cemetery, Dumfries Road (A709), Lockerbie, Dumfries & Galloway, DG11 1HZ | Getting there The Garden of Remembrance is found at the far end of Dryfesdale Cemetery – free car park next to the cemetery; buses 81, 112, 380, 382 and 383; train to Lockerbie station and a 20-minute walk | Hours Unrestricted | Tip Visit the Lockerbie Memorial at Sherwood Crescent, the site where Flight 103 impacted the ground and killed 11 residents (30–32 Sherwood Crescent, Lockerbie, DG11 2DY).

23 Sawney Bean's Cave

A Scottish cannibal who raised an incestuous family

Alexander 'Sawney' Bean was purportedly born in East Lothian during the 16th century. Achieving infamy on the Ayrshire coast, Sawney was a murderous cannibal who became a dark Scottish legend. He was head of a 50-member family clan who killed and ate over 1,000 victims during a 25-year period. His wife, 'Black' Agnes Douglas, shared his abominable inclinations and was accused of being a witch. Living and hiding in a sea cave, accessible only at low tide, Sawney and his clan robbed, murdered and cannibalised their victims.

Sawney and Agnes had six daughters and eight sons who went on to incestuously produce 14 granddaughters and 18 grandsons. The incestuous tribe dismembered corpses and pickled body parts to preserve in their human larder. Limbs often washed up ashore and locals hanged several innocents for alleged crimes. However, when Sawney attacked a couple of newlyweds one night, the wife met a heinous death, but the husband fought back. With the cave discovered, a group of men led by King James arrested Sawney and his clan. The cave was strewn with human limbs and bones, with flesh hanging as if in a butcher's shop. Taken to Edinburgh and executed without trial, male members of the family had their hands, feet and genitals cut off and bled to death. Female members were burned alive.

However, there is no official record of Alexander Bean ever existing. This 'bogeyman' tale might have been propaganda of the English, who portrayed Scots as deviant during the period of Jacobite risings. The monstrous figure of Sawney Bean was probably an English invention. As colonial fiction, 'Sawney' – which is an English derogatory term to describe Scots – was written to show the savagery and uncivilised nature of the Scots. This contrasted with the supposed superior qualities of the English. Whatever the truth, this is another folk tale twisted for political reasons.

Address Bennane Head, Girvan, KA26 0JJ | Getting there Just over 2 miles south of Lendalfoot off the A 77 – cave only accessible at low tide; limited car parking at Girvan Scenic Lookout | Hours Unrestricted, but be aware of tide times | Tip Visit Snib's Cave – home to Henry Torbet (1912–1983) – a former accountant who lived as a hermit for the last 30 years of his life (1 mile south of Sawney Bean's Cave, Girvan, KA26 0LE).

24 Burn O' Vat

A geological quirk with tales of outlaws

In the heart of Royal Deeside is a striking geological quirk. The Burn O'Vat is a deep rocky bowl gouged out by passing water. The Vat Burn runs down from Culblean Hill towards Loch Kinord. Tumbling down a waterfall into an amphitheatre of rocks carved out over millennia, even Queen Victoria managed to climb into the Vat. The Burn O'Vat is part of a trail that takes in the scenic Muir of Dinnet Nature Reserve. Popular as an attraction since Victorian times, the glacier-formed pothole measures 18 metres wide by 13 metres high.

But, the Burn O'Vat has a darker history. Folklore tells of the Vat being used by Rob Roy MacGregor (1671–1734) to hide from authorities. MacGregor was a Jacobite outlaw, who became a Scottish folk hero. Born in the Trossachs, like many Highland clansmen, MacGregor joined the Jacobite movement. Jacobites supported the restoration of King James VII to the throne, after he had abdicated following the Glorious Revolution of 1688. After a loan default and a long-running feud with the Duke of Montrose, MacGregor was branded an outlaw and became a legend in his own lifetime. Yet, it is still unclear whether MacGregor used the Vat as a den.

However, what is clear is that the Vat was used as a hideout for an earlier outlaw – Patrick McGregor (d. 1636). Better known as Gilderoy, meaning 'the Red-haired Lad', he was a leader of a band of 'limmers' or robbers, involved in theft and blackmail, as well as undertaking several 'crewall slauchters', or murders. A shallow depression behind the waterfall in the Vat, where he hid, is known as 'Gilderoy's Cave'. Gilderoy and some of his gang members were caught and tried in Edinburgh in 1636. Found guilty, Gilderoy had a final unenviable accolade of having his gibbet considerably higher than his associates. Hanged by the neck, Gideroy had his head and right hand cut off, and displayed at the port of Edinburgh.

Address Muir of Dinnet Nature Reserve, Dinnet, Aboyne, Aberdeenshire, AB34 5NB | Getting there Car parking available at Muir of Dinnet Nature Reserve off B 9119, then a 20-minute walk (water-resistant footwear recommended) | Hours Unrestricted, but unadvisable to visit during hours of darkness | Tip See the Russell Head, an 1850s effigy of a demonic face carved to haunt a neighbour during a sewer-smell dispute (Russell Head, Provost Skene's House, Marischal Square, Guestrow, Aberdeen, AB10 1AS).

25 The American Monument

Pilgrimage for a double wartime tragedy

On the edge of the Mull of Oa, a rocky peninsula on the island of Islay, is a tall, lonely monument for a double tragedy of World War I. High on a rugged clifftop overlooking the North Channel that separates Scotland from the island of Ireland, the American Monument resembles a windmill shorn of its sails. Erected by the American Red Cross in 1920, the memorial is a silent reminder of the soldiers and sailors who were lost in Islay's cold waters.

On 5 February 1918, the luxury-liner-converted-troopship – SS *Tuscania* – was *en route* from New Jersey to Liverpool. Carrying over 2,000 US servicemen and 60 British crew, she was torpedoed by the German U-boat UB77, some seven miles off the Mull of Oa. Within four hours of the attack, she had sunk, taking over 200 souls to the deep. Many of the bodies washed ashore on Islay. Just over eight months later, on 6 October 1918, and not long before the Armistice of 11 November 1918, a second ship sank. The HMS *Otranto*, heavily laden with US servicemen, collided off Islay in thick fog with another troopship, HMS *Kashmir*. This time, 351 US troops and 80 British crew members lost their lives.

The double tragedy represented the single largest loss of life for the US military since the American Civil War (1861–1865). Many were buried at the military cemetery at Kilchoman, before most of the US victims were repatriated to the USA in the early 1920s. Designed by Robert Walker and 20 metres in height, the American Monument has a door-like commemoration plaque surmounted by an eagle carrying a wreath. With a tribute from US President Woodrow Wilson, the epitaph reads: 'On Fame's Eternal camping ground / Their silent tents are spread / While Glory keeps with solemn round / The bivouac of the dead'. As a place of pilgrimage, it is a solemn marker in the landscape that recalls those who fought a war that should have ended all wars.

Address Mull of Oa, Isle of Islay, Argyll & Bute, PA42 7AU | **Getting there** Car parking at the Mull of Oa RSPB Reserve, then up to a 60-minute walk up to the monument (where the path can be wet and boggy in places) | **Hours** Unrestricted | **Tip** Visit the memorial to Alexander McDougall (1732–1786), an Islay-born man who became George Washington's Major General during the War of Independence, as well as first president of the Bank of New York (off the A846, Port Ellen, Isle of Islay, PA42 7DS).

26 Badbea Clearance Village

Highland Clearances and 'Scottish diaspora'

The Highland Clearances from 1750 to 1860 saw disruption of traditional life and dispossession of land. Farmland was seen as being for profit rather than supporting residents. Intent on maximising their rental yield, landlords moved tenant farmers off Highland farms into coastal crofting communities. Displaced tenants were expected to be employed in fishing, quarrying or the kelp industry.

Landlords were typically clan leaders who, in pre-Clearance times, leased their land to tacksmen, who then sublet to peasant farmers. However, the Highland Clearances saw not only economic change but social engineering in its crudest form. It also ushered in the demise of the clan social system. Later phases of the Clearances saw landowners such as the Duke of Sutherland physically evict people by burning their homes. This draconian policy of expelling people was accompanied by 'assisted emigration' in which landlords paid passage for 'redundant' families to move to North America and Australia. Consequently, the Scottish diaspora today means Scottish culture has not been contained within the borders of Scotland. It has lived on in the minds of migrants and their descendants who are still attached to it.

Overcrowded coastal crofts, failure of the kelp industry, famine caused by potato blight, and landlord greed and debt are all related to the Clearances and the later Scottish diaspora. Yet, displaced Highlanders created small villages such as the now abandoned Badbea (pronounced *Bad-bay*) on a windswept clifftop. With sheep more profitable than people, from 1792 Badbea was a place where people eked out a living. By the 1890s, herring fishing was in decline and families were forced to emigrate. David Sutherland, son of Alexander Sutherland, who had emigrated to New Zealand in 1838, erected a memorial to the people of the Clearances in 1911; the same year the last resident left.

Address Berriedale, Caithness, KW7 6HD (nearest postcode) | **Getting there** Signposted off the A 9 north of Helmsdale; car parking beside road, then a 10-minute walk to the abandoned village (stay clear of the sea cliffs!) | **Hours** Unrestricted | **Tip** Visit the Emigrants Statue commemorating thousands of Highlanders 'cleared' from their ancestral homes during the Highland Clearances (Couper Park, Helmsdale, KW8 6HH).

27 Boleskine House

Home to a malevolent occultist

Nestled along the banks of Loch Ness lies an 18th-century manor house that once belonged to a malevolent sorcerer. Built on the site of a 13th-century church, and with a tunnel linking the house with a nearby graveyard, the first owner was Archibald Fraser (1736–1815). Archibald was the son of Simon Fraser, 11th Lord Lovat, who was nicknamed 'the Fox' for his notorious switching of sides during the Jacobite Uprisings. Absent at the 1746 Battle of Culloden, Simon Fraser was beheaded for treason. It has been reported that his head can be heard rolling down the hallway at Boleskine.

From 1899 to 1913, Boleskine belonged to occultist Aleister Crowley. Described as the 'wickedest man in the world', Cowley practised black magic and founded the religion Thelema. He named himself as the prophet entrusted with guiding humanity into the Aeon of Horus. Crowley used Boleskine's seclusion to summon up satanic spirits through a *grimoire* – a textbook of magic – and his *Sacred Magic of Abramelin the Mage*. While conjuring the 12 Kings and Dukes of Hell, Crowley left for Paris for a meeting with the Golden Dawn, a secret society devoted to the occult. When he was unable to complete the conjuring, demons entered Boleskine – and allegedly have never left!

Tales of hauntings have plagued the house ever since. Hugh Gillies, Crowley's groundskeeper, suffered several personal tragedies. Even Crowley admitted that his black magic had 'got out of hand'. In 1960, the new owner Major Edward Grant committed suicide with a shotgun in Crowley's former bedroom. In 1970, Jimmy Page of legendary rock band Led Zeppelin, and self-confessed 'Crowley enthusiast', bought Boleskine. Leaving the house in the stewardship of his friend Malcolm Dent, reports of supernatural occurrences soon surfaced. After a guest claimed to have been attacked by 'some sort of devil', Dent suggested the house was a place of 'pure evil'.

Address General Wade's Military Road, Inverness, IV2 6XT, +44 (0) 7727 491016, www.boleskinehouse.org | Getting there Boleskine is undergoing restoration – see website for entry requirements; 1.5 miles north of Foyers, off B 852 | Hours Check website for seasonal opening times | Tip Take a trip on Beastie Boats and explore 'Nessie's Lair' – the deepest part of Loch Ness, where the Loch Ness Monster legend was born (Foyers Pier, Inverness, IV2 6YB, www.beastieboats.com).

28 Commando Memorial

'United we conquer'

Tasked with guarding the memory of British Commando Forces is the iconic Commando Memorial. Gazing out towards the majestic peaks of Ben Nevis and Aonach Mòr, across the River Spean valley, the memorial offers an emotional heart to the Highlands. At the behest of Winston Churchill after Dunkirk in 1940, Commandoes became the elite fighting unit of the British Army. Based at nearby Achnacarry Castle, the Lochaber region was used as a highly intensive training ground for the Commandoes. This was their country.

Sculpted in 1952 by Scott Sutherland (1910–1994), the 17-foot memorial takes the form of three bronze life-size commandos in World War II uniforms, including cap comforters, ammunition pouches and rifles. The soldier at the front is Gunner Jack Lewington (1915–1996), who was wounded during operations in 1944 at Flushing, Holland. Jack returned to his police officer role in Berkshire after the war. Sergeant Major Sidney Hewlett (1911–1983) is also thought to be depicted at the memorial. Born in Barry in South Wales, and wounded in 1941, Sidney trained Commandoes at the Commando Mountain Warfare Training Centre. The final solider is apparently Captain Frank Nicholls of No. 7 Commando, later renamed Layforce. Frank was killed in action by a bomb dropped by a Japanese biplane on 11 May 1942. He has no known grave.

Over 1,700 Commandoes were killed during the war, with eight Victoria Crosses awarded to Commandoes for valour. Today, the Special Air Service (SAS) and Special Boat Service (SBS) – the UK's special forces – can trace their origins to the Commandoes of World War II. Many Royal Marine Commandoes who have died in other theatres of war, including the Falklands and conflicts in Iraq and Afghanistan, have their ashes scattered at the memorial. With the epitaph of 'United we conquer', the impressive memorial is a poignant reminder that society is still fragile.

Address Spean Bridge, PH34 4EG | Getting there Car parking available next to the memorial, just off the A 82/B 8004; buses 43 and 510b to Spean Bridge (Braelea), then a 25-minute walk | Hours Unrestricted | Tip Visit the Lochalsh War Memorial, a remote Highland commemoration where a quarter of the fallen are named MacRae (off the A87, Balmacara, Kyle, IV40 8DH, nearest postcode).

29 Culloden

Last pitched battle fought in Britain

On 16 April 1746 at Culloden Moor, the last pitched battle on British soil took place. Over 1,600 men died and the final chapter in a sporadic civil war closed. Often portrayed as a conflict between the Scots and English, Culloden was a fight between Jacobitism (a movement supporting restoration of the House of Stuart and King James, rendered in Latin as *Jacobus*) and British government forces.

In 1688, King James VII of Scotland (II of England) was deposed by Protestant William of Orange, fearful that James was starting a Catholic dynasty. Efforts to restore Jacobitism led to many conflicts. In 1745, Charles Edward Stuart – the 'Young Pretender' or 'Bonnie Prince Charlie' – led an army of Highlanders, French, Irish and some English to take on King George II. On 4 December 1745, they reached Derby. Thinking that English support was weak and French allies were unable to invade, Bonnie Prince Charlie retreated. Despite a victory at the Battle of Falkirk Muir on 17 January 1746, the Young Pretender did not capitalise. Retreating to Inverness, on boggy land called Culloden Moor, exhausted and outnumbered Jacobite forces were defeated by the army of the Duke of Cumberland. Prince Charlie escaped to France, but brutal reprisals by 'Butcher Cumberland' saw the end of the clan system and beginning of the 'Highland Clearances'.

Unaware that Welsh Jacobites were rising, and English Jacobite support was growing, and that the royal court in London was panicking, some say if Prince Charlie had pressed on from Derby, King George II would have fled; the English and French would have avoided 70 years of conflict; the English would have not had to raise colonial taxes; and the Americans would have had no cause to fight for independence; nor would the French Revolution have happened. Alternative histories aside, visitors today can visit the battlefield and wonder – *what if?*

Address Culloden Battlefield & Visitor Centre, Inverness, IV2 5EU, www.nts.org.uk/visit/places/culloden | Getting there Culloden is 5 miles east of Inverness, off the A 9/B 9006 – follow the brown signs to Culloden; hourly bus service from Inverness (journey time 30 minutes) | Hours Visitor Centre daily 9am–4pm; battlefield unrestricted | Tip Visit Old High Church Kirkyard and see the execution spot of captured Jacobite soldiers from Culloden (Church Street, Inverness, IV1 1EY).

30 Cuween Chambered Cairn

Ancient burial chamber under a hill

Orkney is an archipelago off the north coast of Scotland and has been inhabited for over 8,500 years. The rich history of bygone settlements offers a fascinating window into life (and death) millennia ago in Scotland's remote northern islands. After the last Ice Age, Mesolithic hunter-gatherers gradually transitioned to farming and settled in small agricultural communities. It was during the Neolithic period, around 3000 B.C., that many of Orkney's ancient sites were built. Some of them still survive today. These include Skara Brae, a domestic settlement, and the Standing Stones of Stenness, a circular henge that is older than both Stonehenge in England and the Great Pyramids of Giza in Egypt.

However, it is Neolithic burial chambered cairns that dominate Orkney's ancient landscape. These mysterious venerable tombs show how funerary rituals were performed by people long past. The use of astronomical calendars and alignment of the tombs with the moon and lunar cycles offer tantalising clues about prehistoric inhabitants. The enigmatic structures are as intriguing as they are engineering feats.

One such burial site is Cuween Hill, perched on the hillside above the Bay of Firth, near Finstown. First excavated in 1901, the tomb forms a large chamber and four side-cells to place corpses. Eight sets of human remains were discovered in the tomb, as well as the bones of 24 dogs. Canine remains suggest evocative and spiritual burial rituals, where animals were seen as a totem – a spirit being or symbol that accompany the dead into the afterlife. A reconstruction of a dog from Cuween by Edinburgh University in 2019 showed a dog the size of a large collie with the appearance of a European grey wolf. Today, visitors to Cuween can enter the tomb the same way as our Neolithic ancestors did – crawling on hands and knees through a narrow, and often muddy, entrance way.

Address Old Finstown Road, Firth, Orkney, KW17 2EJ, +44 (0) 1856 841815, www.orkney.com/listings/cuween-cairn | Getting there Small free car park; 10-minute walk up steep hill, off Old Finstown Road | Hours Unrestricted | Tip Visit nearby Maeshowe Chambered Cairn, a 5,000-year-old tomb with runic graffiti left by Vikings (Maeshowe Visitor Centre, Ireland Road, Stenness, Orkney, KW16 3LB).

31 Eagle's Rock Memorial

Mysterious death of a libertine prince

At 1.42pm on 25 August 1942, a Short Sunderland seaplane mysteriously crashed into Eagle's Rock in Caithness. Flying from Invergordon to RAF Reykjavik, 14 out of the 15 men on board were killed. The victims included Prince George, Duke of Kent, who was an RAF Air Commodore on a mission to Iceland. Prince George (1902–1942) was the fourth son of King George V and Queen Mary, and brother to Kings Edward VIII and George VI. The sole survivor was Andrew Jack (1922–1978), the aircraft's Wireless Operator/Air Gunner, who was found a day after the accident.

Why the seaplane crashed into a hillside in daylight with good visibility is a source of contention. The official inquiry concluded an error of navigation. Yet, tales of an unaccounted extra person aboard the plane remain. Some suggest it was Nazi Rudolf Hess, who had made a solo flight to Scotland in 1941 for supposed peace talks. Yet, Hess died in Spandau Prison in 1987. Other rumours suggest the curious passenger was the boyfriend of married Prince George. Fifth in line to the throne, bisexual George was a drug-taking prince whose short life was filled with debauchery. He dallied with, among others, a male Prussian relative, a Parisian prostitute, Cambridge spy Anthony Blunt, and Margaret, Duchess of Argyll – a lady known for her 'fragile morals'. Some suggest the British secret service arranged the crash to cover up the prince's extravagances, as well as an illegitimate son.

However, Andrew Jack claimed on his deathbed that Prince George was flying the doomed plane and confirmed a person was aboard, who should not have been. He also claimed he pulled Prince George out of the pilot position and placed his body away from the wreckage. In 1946, two memorials were erected: a Latin cross that commemorates all victims, and a smaller stone away from the crash site marking where Prince George's body was found.

Address Eagle's Rock Memorial, Berriedale Water, Braemore, Caithness, KW6 6EX (nearest postcode) | **Getting there** The memorial is in a remote location with rough tracks; National Grid Reference ND 11059 28377, north of Berriedale Water, about 3 miles west of Borgue, 4 miles south-west of Dunbeath | **Hours** Unrestricted | **Tip** Visit another 'Eagle Rock', where a weather-worn carving of an eagle is thought to date from the Roman occupation of Caledonia (Eagle Rock, Cramond, Edinburgh, EH30 9TQ).

32 Flannan Isles Lighthouse

Vanishing of 'three dead men'

'A dreadful accident has happened at the Flannans,' reported the SS *Archtor*, as it sailed past the Flannan Isles and saw no light from the lighthouse on Eilean Mòr. It was 15 December 1900, and the lighthouse had only been operational for a year. As a small island group west of the Isle of Lewis, the Flannan Isles or the 'Seven Hunters', was home to a 76-foot lighthouse perched atop a 196-foot cliff. Three lighthouse keepers – James Ducat (43), Thomas Marshall (28) and Donald McArthur (40) – manned the remote outpost.

On 26 December, the *Hesperus* sailed to investigate and found the island in a mysterious state of disarray. Relief keeper Joseph Moore found no welcome from the three residents, no flag on the flagstaff, doors to the compound closed, beds unmade, and the clock stopped. A set of oilskins was found, meaning that one of the keepers had left without his rain gear. Log entries suggested a storm, but no storm had been reported by the authorities. The three keepers had simply vanished. Only a canary in a cage was found alive.

On the western side of the isle, storm damage was clear. Moore assumed the three keepers had succumbed to rogue waves from a heavy sea while trying to secure the west landing mooring and its equipment. However, without a clear explanation, speculation mounted that foul play may have played a role. Tales about McArthur's short temper and violent behaviour surfaced and led to dubious rumours of a possible fight between the keepers. One theory is that McArthur killed Ducat and Marshall, then committed suicide by jumping into the sea.

The bodies of the three lightkeepers were never found and the mystery stays unsolved today. With no trace of 'three dead men', the mystery has inspired popular culture, including the chamber opera *The Lighthouse* (1979), Wilfrid Gibson's poem 'Flannan Isle' (1912), and the movie *The Vanishing* (2018).

Address Eilean Mòr, Flannan Isles, Outer Hebrides | **Getting there** The only way to Eilean Mòr is by boat; for operators, see www.visitouterhebrides.co.uk – landing on the Flannans is not recommended (the lighthouse, automated in 1971, is uninhabited) | **Hours** Unrestricted, but best to visit during summer months | **Tip** Visit the *Time & Tide Bell*, a sculpture offering warnings of modern climate change (Bosta Beach, Great Bernera, Isle of Lewis, HS52 9LZ, www.timeandtidebell.org).

33 Glencoe Massacre

Treacherous clan rivalry leads to slaughter

Glencoe is a majestic, steep-sided valley in the heart of the Highlands that has a haunting history. In 1692, English troops massacred 38 men, women and children of the MacDonald clan. Many more succumbed to exposure as they evaded the onslaught. The bloodbath culminated in a 200-year inter-clan feud between the MacDonalds and Campbells. Yet, the massacre was also a plot to bring Highland clans in line behind King William III/II and suppress its 'troublesome' residents to ensure English dominance.

In August 1691, King William III/II offered to pardon all clans who fought against him during the Jacobite Uprisings. Conditional upon allegiance to the king, clan chief Alastair MacDonald arrived at Inverary five days late to take the oath, having mistakenly travelled to Fort William. Secretary of State for Scotland – Sir John Dalrymple – wanted to set an example to those clans not taking allegiance. Despite the MacDonalds taking the oath, albeit late, they were chosen for punishment. On 1 February 1692, under the command of a bankrupt alcoholic – Captain Robert Campbell – 130 English troops were billeted in Glencoe with the MacDonalds. The order for Captain Campbell came to 'fall upon the Rebells… and putt all to sword under seventy'. At 5am on 13 February 1692, the slaughter began with a man called Maclain killed, before troops traversed the glen and crofts slaying anyone under the age of 70.

The infamy of the massacre is perhaps less to do with the numbers killed, but more to do with abuse of hospitality offered by the MacDonalds, a cornerstone of Highland life. A public outcry followed, while a Parliamentary Commission decided the killings as 'murder under trust'. Dalrymple and the king avoided any real repercussions. The blame was laid upon the Campbell clan, and a local inn today still displays a (tongue-in-cheek) sign: 'No hawkers or Campbells'.

Address Glencoe Visitor Centre, near Glencoe Village, Lochaber, PH49 4HX, +44 (0) 1855 811307, www.nts.org.uk/visit/places/glencoe | **Getting there** Located on the A 82 on the right, 1 mile after Glencoe village; buses between Glasgow & Fort William stop in Glencoe, then a 25-minute walk | **Hours** Daily 2 Jan–31 Mar 10am–4pm, 1 Apr–26 Oct 9.30am–5pm | **Tip** Visit the Glencoe Folk Museum and see weapons used to suppress Jacobite sympathisers (Main Street, Glencoe, PH49 4HS, www.glencoemuseum.com).

34 Glenfinnan Monument

Clansmen killed during the Jacobite Uprising

At the head of Loch Shiel, framed by majestic Highland scenery, is the Glenfinnan Monument. At 59 feet tall, a kilted Highlander stands atop this striking architectural folly. It is a tribute to the zeal of clansmen who fought and died in that doomed crusade – the 1745 Jacobite Uprising. The monument was erected when Jacobitism was no longer considered a political threat to the Hanoverian monarchy.

On 19 August 1745, Prince Charles Edward Stuart, otherwise known as 'Bonnie Prince Charlie' or the 'Young Pretender', rowed up Loch Shiel to Glenfinnan. He wanted to regain the British Crown for the Stuarts and restore his father James VIII as King of Scotland, England and Ireland, and himself as the Prince Regent. Seeking Highland clan military support, Prince Charles was met by hundreds of men from Clans Cameron, MacDonnell and McPhee. A ceremony to mark the 1745 Uprising was held near Glenfinnan Church and a Prince's standard raised to mark Charles' claim to the throne. With advances all the way to Derby and becoming tantalisingly close to victory, the Uprising saw its final defeat at the Battle of Culloden in 1746, where many of the clansmen were slain. Prince Charles evaded capture and made his way to France in 1746. He never set foot on Scottish soil again.

Highland life was never the same after the Uprising. The English establishment tried to destroy the archaic clan system with the Highland Clearances (1750–1860). It ushered in a period of self-interest, evictions and forced emigration. In 1815, Alexander MacDonald built the Glenfinnan Monument, funded by family wealth derived from the slave trade. In 1835, the statue of an anonymous Highlander was added. Since 1938, the memorial has been in the care of the National Trust for Scotland. The nearby Glenfinnan Viaduct and 'Hogwarts Express' will be recognised by Harry Potter movie fans.

Address Glenfinnan Monument & Visitor Centre, Glenfinnan, PH37 4LT, +44 (0) 1397 722250, www.nts.org.uk/visit/places/glenfinnan-monument | Getting there Monument is free to view, but fee is payable to climb the tower; bus 500 from Fort William; train to Glenfinnan station, then a 15-minute walk; part of the scenic West Highland Line from Glasgow to Mallaig | Hours Unrestricted, but see website for Visitor Centre hours | Tip See The Prince's Cairn, the spot where Bonnie Prince Charlie finally left Scotland for France in 1746 (by the A 830, 4 miles west of Lochailort, PH38 4NA).

35 Gloup Disaster Memorial

A historic sea-faring tragedy

In the Shetland Islands, on the island of Yell in the village of Gloup, is a memorial to a tragic fishing disaster. On 20–21 July 1881, many anglers perished when an unexpected northerly summer storm hit a fishing fleet. At the time, fishing was conducted in traditional boats known as *sixareens* or *sixerns*. Rowed by six men, these large open clinker-built vessels had six compartments for stowing fish, provisions and tackle. Known as 'Haaf' fishing, which involved the whole community in processing the fish, lines of up to seven miles were used to catch cod, halibut and other deep-water fish. At its peak, Haaf fishing employed over 3,000 men across Shetland, where *sixareens* were skippered by experienced navigators.

Gloup – a common Scottish placename meaning 'sea jet' – was the second largest Haaf station in Shetland. When the fishing fleet left Gloup in July 1881, anglers were unaware of an impending calamity. With no warning, the storm struck, and 10 *sixareens* foundered with a loss of 58 souls. One boat did miraculously escape and rode out the storm. More than half of the lost anglers and six of the sunken boats came from Gloup. Some 34 widows and 85 children were left destitute, though an emergency fund was set up.

Some 50 years before, on 16 July 1832, a fishing disaster had also occurred. Known as the 'Bad Day', a similar summer storm hit a Haaf fleet of *sixareens* off the west coast of Shetland. The carnage saw 17 boats lost, with the death toll reaching 105 men from various parts of Shetland.

After the Gloup Disaster, Haaf fishing dwindled as herrings became the main catch and *sixareens* were replaced by safer boats. The Gloup Disaster was the last tragedy involving *sixareens*. In 1981, to mark the disaster centenary, a monument was erected in Gloup. It portrays a woman with babe in arms gazing out to sea for the men who never returned.

Address Off B9083, Easterhouse, Gloup, Yell, Shetland Islands, ZE2 9DD | Getting there Road leading to the memorial is difficult to navigate after dark; small car park available | Hours Unrestricted | Tip Visit the Dutchman's Leap, where legend suggests a Dutch angler and his Shetland pony tumbled down a cliff to their doom (Knab Road, Lerwick, Shetland Mainland, ZE1 0YB).

36 Flora MacDonald's Grave

Hero of the Highlands

Dominating Kilmuir Cemetery on the Isle of Skye is the Celtic cross gravestone of Flora MacDonald. Born in 1722 on South Uist in the Outer Hebrides, Flora became a Jacobite hero who morphed into Scottish romanticism. When visiting Benbecula, Flora met Prince Charles Edward Stuart, otherwise known as Jacobite leader 'Bonnie Prince Charlie'. After the Jacobite Uprising in 1745 and their final defeat at the Battle of Culloden in 1746, Stuart was on the run from English forces. To help him evade capture, Flora agreed to help Stuart escape Scotland. As he was a very slight man, Flora disguised him as an Irish housekeeper and called him Betty Burke. Camouflaged from the English, Flora led 'Betty' and his party and sailed to Skye.

Stuart eventually escaped to France. Flora never saw him again but was arrested for her role in the escape and sent to the Tower of London. In 1747, Flora was pardoned after aristocratic sympathisers campaigned for her release. In 1750, she married Allan MacDonald but with poor harvests and the Highland Clearances, they emigrated to America in 1774. With the American War of Independence beginning in 1775, Allan joined the Royal Highland Emigrants and fought with the British. He was taken prisoner and only released in 1783. Flora was interrogated, and her property and belongings confiscated. She returned to Britain in 1779. During the voyage back, her ship was attacked by pirates, and she suffered injuries during onboard hostilities.

Flora achieved celebrity status, causing Dr Samuel Johnson, the famous essayist, to remark 'a name will be mentioned in history and if courage and fidelity be virtues, mentioned with honour'. Flora died in 1790, aged 68, and was buried in a shroud made from a sheet that Bonnie Prince Charlie had slept in. Her original gravestone was chipped away by trophy hunters and replaced in the 19th century.

Address Kilmuir Cemetery, Portree, Isle of Skye, IV51 9UE | Getting there Car parking at the nearby Skye Museum of Island Life – follow gravel path from the museum to the cemetery; some steps and uneven ground | Hours Unrestricted | Tip Nearby in Kilmuir Cemetery is the headstone of iconic British fashion designer Alexander McQueen, who sadly died by suicide aged 40 in 2010.

37 The Ghost Village

Splendid isolation abandoned for modernity

Lying in the North Atlantic is the outpost of St Kilda. An archipelago of four islands – Hirta, Soay, Boreray and Dùn – St Kilda is one of the few World Heritage Sites in existence awarded dual status for both natural and cultural significance. With Europe's highest sea cliff, the islands are home to the continent's largest colony of seabirds. Species unique to St Kilda include sheep, mice and wrens. Today, St Kilda is a National Nature Reserve, as well as home to a military radar station.

St Kilda was part of the Lordship of the Isles from 1498 to 1930, then a property of the MacLeods of Dunvegan. Inhabited since around 3000 B.C., Hirta – the largest island in the group – is now abandoned. The island's distance from the rest of the Outer Hebrides allowed for a unique subsistence economy. In the late 17th century Hirta had 180 residents, but by 1851 the population had dwindled to 112. In 1852, 36 residents emigrated to Australia, financed by the Highland & Island Emigration Society. Islanders had a tough life, surviving on seabirds, oatmeal and salted fowl. With few fruits or vegetables, and limited healthcare and education, by 1911 only 74 people remained.

Tourism in the 1870s punctured the splendid isolation of Hirta. In 1901, a new pier allowed larger ships to disembark visitors. World War I saw the installation of defences and young men leave for military service. After the war, with many men not returning, as well as an outbreak of Spanish Flu, the population was only 36 by 1930. Fearing for their survival, at the Islanders' own request they were evacuated, and on 29 August 1930 the final residents boarded HMS *Harebell* and travelled to Lochaline. They left in their now-ruined cottages a bowl of oats and an open Bible, an island tradition. The last person to live on Hirta, Rachel Johnson, died in 2016 after settling in Clydebank. She had been eight years old when she left.

Address Hirta Village, St Kilda, Outer Hebrides | **Getting there** The only way to Hirta is by boat; for operators, see www.nts.org.uk/visit/places/st-kilda | **Hours** Unrestricted, but best to visit during summer months | **Tip** Stay in a formerly abandoned Hebridean village with traditional Highlander blackhouses (Gearrannan Blackhouse Village, 5a Gearrannan, Carloway, Isle of Lewis, HS2 9AL, www.gearrannan.com).

38 Gruinard Island

'Anthrax Island' and cakes of death

Gruinard (pronounced GRIN-yard) Island was described by Dean Munro (a 16th-century clergyman) as 'guid for fostering of thieves and rebellis' (good for hiding thieves and rebels). In the late 1780s, Gruinard was used for grazing sheep. But in 1881, the population was only six people. Without an established populace, Rosalynd Maitland bought the island in 1926, and bequeathed it to her niece Molly Dunphie, a friend of Winston Churchill.

By 1942, Churchill feared Nazi Germany was developing biological weapons. In response, Operation Vegetarian was instigated by Porton Down, the UK's controversial defence laboratory. The plan was to poison German livestock by dropping linseed cakes laced with *Bacillus anthracis* – anthrax – onto the German countryside. The idea was for the 'cakes' to be eaten by cattle and sheep, which were then consumed by humans, leading to widespread death and starvation. Requisitioned by the British government, Gruinard Island was 'sacrificed' to test the biowarfare. A virulent strain of anthrax – 'Vollum 14578' – was detonated across the island. Documentary evidence declassified in 1997 shows how tethered sheep died within days of exposure, with carcasses incinerated. The experiments concluded that anthrax would completely pollute German areas, making them uninhabitable for decades afterwards. Ready for deployment with five million 'cakes' in early 1944, the D-Day landings caused Operation Vegetarian to be abandoned.

With Gruinard poisoned, it was not until 1981 that activists under Operation Dark Harvest demanded government decontaminate the island. In 1986, a clean-up began, and in 1990 Gruinard was considered safe. It was resold to heirs of the original owner for £500. In 2022, the island was almost entirely burned by a wildfire. Today, visitors can gaze upon the 'forbidden island' where mass death through poison was contemplated.

Address Achnasheen, IV22 2NQ | Getting there The island can be viewed from the coast along the A 832; car park about 1 mile west of Mungasdale | Hours Unrestricted | Tip Visit Loch Eriboll, one of the deepest sea lochs in Scotland, where 33 Nazi U-boats surrendered at the end of World War II (Loch Eriboll viewpoint, off A838, Heilam, Lairg, IV27 4UL).

39 Iolaire Memorial

Crowning sorrow of World War I

At 1.55am on 1 January 1919, the 'crowning sorrow' of World War I hit the Isle of Lewis. HMY *Iolaire* (Gaelic for 'Eagle'), a former aristocrat's yacht built in 1881, was carrying home sailors from the war. In gale force winds and heavy seas, it struck the 'Beasts of Holm', a group of protruding rocks less than a mile from Stornoway Harbour. The usual ferry to the Isle, the SS *Sheila*, was already at capacity. So, the Admiralty drafted in *Iolaire*, which it had requisitioned in 1915, to help with the passage. Docked at Kyle, the *Iolaire* clipped the pier, and some refused to board her. Yet, *Iolaire* departed Kyle overloaded and those aboard would have seen Stornoway just before disaster struck.

Just 50 feet from shore, *Iolaire* sank with the loss of 205 men. Of the victims, 181 died on the very shores of the island they called home. With bodies washing ashore for some time after the tragedy, 56 were never recovered, and the island ran out of coffins. There were 75 survivors. After the sinking, a public inquiry found inadequate care had been taken during the approach to the harbour. It also found insufficient lifeboats and lifebelts on board for the number of passengers. Despite the provision of lifesaving equipment being legally addressed by the 1912 *Titanic* disaster, it had not been implemented due to the war. It was not until 1929 that full implementation of lifesaving equipment was enforced by law.

With post-war economic decline and the effects of the Spanish Flu epidemic, the *Iolaire* calamity, together with war losses, the Isle was robbed of many young men. A disaster fund was set up for widows and families, which offered more than war widow pensions. A memorial was erected in 1958 and the *Iolaire* is still an overwhelming event in Western Isles' history. Apart from the *Titanic*, it is the worst peacetime maritime disaster in UK history for a British ship.

Address Sandwick, Isle of Lewis, Outer Hebrides, HS2 0AQ | Getting there Free car parking; main ferry crossing is Ullapool to Stornoway; flights to Stornoway by Loganair or Hebridean Air Services | Hours Unrestricted | Tip Visit the Gress Raiders Memorial, where returning servicemen found their crofts confiscated by Lord Leverhulme after World War I (follow brown sign for 'The Land Struggle', off B895, Gress, Isle of Lewis, HS2 0LQ).

40 Massacre Cave

Mass murder of MacDonalds

Eigg is one of the Small Isles in the Scottish Inner Hebrides, south of its neighbour Skye. As the most eco-friendly island in the UK, its tranquil setting masks a harrowing history. Yet, deep within a rocky cavern on Eigg's south coast occurred one of Scotland's bloodiest mass murders. With its narrow entrance, the Cave of Francis or 'Uamh Fhraing' (in Gaelic) saw almost the entire island population massacred in 1577.

The killings were part of a generation-long feud between Clan MacDonald (from Eigg) and Clan MacLeod (from Skye). After a storm, some MacLeod men landed on a small islet near Eigg. After helping themselves to cattle, they began molesting local girls. The MacDonalds were furious and crossed to the islet and dispatched the MacLeods. They reserved the worst fate for the son of the MacLeod chieftain, by breaking his limbs and casting him adrift in a boat without oars. His death was long and painful. Chief MacLeod vowed revenge on the MacDonalds. He sent a fleet of warriors to Eigg, but their galleys were spotted. Fearing bloodshed, up to 400 MacDonald men, women and children fled and hid in the Cave of Francis.

When the MacLeods landed, they found only an elderly lady who refused to say anything of her fellow islanders' hiding place. After destroying all the MacDonalds' homes, the MacLeods set back off to Skye. However, at sea they spotted a scout near the cave – who was seeing if the MacLeods had left. The MacLeods returned and blocked the cave's entrance with flammable material. They then set it alight, and all the trapped MacDonalds suffocated by smoke and perished. In the 19th century, Victorian tourists took MacDonald bones as souvenirs, including Sir Walter Scott, who claimed a skull. While most victims were buried in local graveyards after the massacre, bones of a 16-year-old MacDonald victim were found in the cave by tourists in 2016.

Address Isle of Eigg, PH42 4RL | **Getting there** Coastal path to the cave is marked with purple waymarkers, but these are easy to miss; 15-minute walk from Eigg ferry terminal | **Hours** Unrestricted, but beware of incoming tides | **Tip** Visit the ruined Trumpan Church where in 1578 the MacDonalds took revenge for the cave massacre and set fire to the MacLeod church with the congregation inside (Waternish, Isle of Skye, IV55 8GW).

41_Oil Rig 'Graveyard'

Industrial ruins and economic ghosts

The Cromarty Firth in north-east Scotland offers a sheltered harbour guarded by two headlands nicknamed 'The Sutors'. The Firth, once home to the British Atlantic Fleet, was the scene of the Invergordon Mutiny in 1931. Over a pay dispute, Royal Navy sailors refused military orders. With dramatic, striking scenery, the Firth is a Special Protection Area for wildlife conservation. Dolphins call the Firth home, while basking sharks are regular visitors.

Yet, among the beauty of the natural habitat, the Cromarty Firth is the haunt of exiled oil rigs. Up to a dozen rusted rigs are safely 'parked' within anchorage areas. In water depths of up to 131 feet, the old oil rigs are either hot stacked – that is, with a skeleton crew onboard and power on – or cold stacked, with no crew and the power switched off. Against the arrestive coastal and rural landscape, the oil rigs offer a surreal juxtaposition of the natural vista against manufactured machines.

As oil prices crashed due to global economic turbulence in the late 2010s, drilling for oil in the North Sea became less profitable. With the nearby city of Aberdeen as the oil capital of Europe, Scotland suffered a significant loss of national revenue resulting in oil industry decline. As the rigs are hauled into harbour, the mammoth vessels are a poignant reminder of a rich industrial past.

These industrial ruins anchored alone in the Firth are haunted by the decay of heavy industry. Scotland is now in a post-industrial era where its industrial prominence in shipbuilding, coal mining and oil drilling has waned.

Some oil rigs in this 'graveyard' will ultimately be decommissioned and scrapped. Others will be brought back to mechanical life and once again drill in the deep depths of the North Sea. Whatever the case, the retired oil rigs serve as warnings from history of economic perils and industrial fragility.

Address Port of Invergordon, Shore Road, Invergordon, IV18 0HD | Getting there Train to Invergordon station – rigs can be viewed onshore along the B 9163 towards Cromarty, or along the B 817 towards Barbaraville (number of anchored rigs will vary) | Hours Unrestricted | Tip Visit the Piper Alpha Memorial Garden, commemorating 165 men killed in the world's worst oil rig disaster in 1988 in the North Sea (Hazelhead Park, Aberdeen, AB15 8BJ).

42 Royal Oak Memorial Garden

Reflecting the sad loss of naval souls

Scapa Flow in Orkney was a hugely important naval base for the Royal Navy during the two world wars. It was a well-defended naval anchorage. Yet, on 14 October 1939, a German U-boat – U-47 – managed to manoeuvre underwater defences. As U-47 made its way through the Kirk Sound channel between the islands of Lamb Holm and Mainland, into Scapa Flow, it fired six torpedoes at HMS *Royal Oak*.

Anchored as a training ship, HMS *Royal Oak* was built in 1916 as a Revenge-class battleship. Of the ship's complement of 1,234 men and boys (some as young as 14 years old, as many lied about their age to enlist), 834 were killed in the attack, including over 100 sea boys aged under 18. Most of the souls went to the deep with their ship, while 26 victims were recovered and buried at nearby Lyness. Captain Günther Prien of U-47 became a celebrity in Germany and the first submariner to be awarded the Knight's Cross. After the raid, Winston Churchill ordered advanced defences for Scapa Flow. The Churchill Barriers were built as four protective causeways, which now serve as link roadways for the islands. In 2010, an understated yet poignant memorial garden for HMS *Royal Oak* was unveiled at the head of Scapa Flow. Other tragedies are also remembered at the garden. On 9 July 1917, while anchored at Scapa Flow, a devastating accidental explosion from faulty cordite blew HMS *Vanguard* apart. Only two of the 845 crew aboard survived. Commander Edwin Dunning is also commemorated at the garden. He was killed on 7 August 1917 when making one of the first attempts to land a biplane on HMS *Furious* in Scapa Flow. Both wrecks of HMS *Vanguard* and *Royal Oak* are designated war graves under the 1986 Protection of Military Remains Act, making unofficial diving illegal. A green buoy in Scapa Flow marks the sorrowful spot where HMS *Royal Oak* sank.

Address Scapa Bay, Kirkwall, Orkney, KW15 1SD | Getting there Garden is near the harbourmaster's depot | Hours Unrestricted | Tip Visit the Italian Chapel, ornately built from Nissen huts by Italian PoWs transported to Orkney to help construct the Churchill Barriers (Lamb Holm, Orkney, KW17 2SF).

43 Ruthven Barracks

'Let every man seek his own safety'

Dominating the head of the Spey Valley stand the remains of Ruthven Barracks. On a prominent mound visible for miles around, the barracks were built on the site of medieval castles. Built by King George I in 1721 following the 1715 Jacobite Uprising, the garrison housed infantry to police the Highlands and enforce the 1716 Disarming Act. Jacobitism is often seen as Scottish nationalism. It included an aristocratic rejection of an increasing unitary state, as well as feudal opposition to capitalism. It fought for a change in the monarch, advocating the restoration of the Catholic House of Stuart to the British throne.

Doomed to fail in their political cause, a 300-strong Jacobite cadre attacked Ruthven Barracks in 1745. A force of only 12 Redcoats, commanded by Sergeant Molloy, successfully fought them off with the loss of just one man. Newly promoted Lieutenant Molloy saw another Jacobite attack in February 1746. This time, the Jacobites won, and the garrison surrendered. After their final defeat at the Battle of Culloden in April 1746, over 3,000 Jacobites rallied at Ruthven Barracks. They intended to fight on. However, a message arrived from Jacobite leader Bonnie Prince Charlie. It simply read, 'Let every man seek his own safety in the best way he can'. Setting fire to the barracks, the Jacobites dispersed across the Highlands to evade a government intent on supressing them – once and for all.

The first castle on the site was built in 1229. By 1371, Alexander Stewart – the Wolf of Badenoch – who reportedly dabbled in the black arts, here. In 1394, a visitor to the castle dressed all in black challenged Stewart to a game of chess. Allegedly, in the morning there was nobody in the castle left alive. Stewart had reputedly played with Lucifer. The spectre of Stewart apparently still haunts the place, as he continues his chess game with the devil.

Address Near Kingussie, PH21 1NR | Getting there Located 1 mile from Kingussie, signposted from A 9 & A 86; limited free parking | Hours Unrestricted | Tip Visit Fort George, one of the most imposing fortifications in Europe, built in the wake of the 1746 Battle of Culloden (near Ardersier, Inverness, IV2 7TD).

44_Scapa Flow

Murdered sailor is last to die from World War I

Scapa Flow has played an important role in travel, trade and conflict for centuries. Meaning 'bay of the long isthmus' from Old Norse, Vikings anchored their longships within the sheltered waters of Scapa Flow. Up to 1946, it was the site of the UK's chief naval base during the world wars. However, Scapa Flow as a body of water is best known for being the graveyard of an entire navy.

The Imperial German Navy High Seas Fleet, consisting of 74 ships, were interned by the Armistice of 11 November 1918. While terms of formal surrender of Germany during World War I were negotiated in Paris, her navy had to disarm and sail into internment. Scapa Flow was the location, and the German armada anchored around the island of Cava in the Orkney Isles. Mutiny had gripped German naval bases, and morale was low among German sailors. A skeleton crew to man the German fleet was left in Orkney as 17,675 sailors were repatriated to Germany. Fearing Britain would seize the ships, or the German government might reject the Treaty of Versailles and resume the war, and the ships be used against Germany, commander Rear Admiral Ludwig von Reuter decided to scuttle the fleet.

On 21 June 1919, Reuter sent a command to sink his ships, of which 52 sank to the depths of Scapa Flow. The Royal Marines, treating the incident as hostile, opened fire on unarmed escaping sailors. Eight Germans were killed aboard lifeboats rowing for land. After the peace treaty was signed, a ninth German sailor – 19-year-old Kuno Eversberg – was attacked on board HMS *Resolution* on 24 June 1919. He died of peritonitis on 29 June 1919. James Wooley, a 19-year-old Royal Navy deserter was tried for murder but a verdict of 'Not Proven' was given. Eversberg's was the last death directly inflicted by World War I. Today, Scapa Flow is a diving destination, and a museum showcases the location during the world war periods.

Address Scapa Flow Museum, Lyness, Hoy, Orkney, KW16 3NT, +44 (0) 1856 791300, www.orkneymuseums.co.uk | **Getting there** For directions, including ferry timetables to Hoy, see www.orkneymuseums.co.uk/our-museums/scapa-flow-museum | **Hours** See website for seasonal opening times | **Tip** Visit the grave of Kuno Eversberg, the murdered sailor at Scapa Flow and last to die as a result of World War I (Lyness Royal Naval Cemetery, off B9047, Island of Hoy, Orkney, KW16 3NT).

45 St Columba's Well

Saintly miracles and an early 'Loch Ness Monster'

Around the year A.D. 565, Saint Columba travelled from Iona up the Great Glen to visit Brude, a king of the Picts. As an Irish abbot, Columba's mission was to convert the Picts of Scotland from paganism to Christianity. Columba was born on 7 December 521 (d. 597) to Fedlimid and Eithne of the Cenél Conaill in Gartan, now modern County Donegal in Ireland. He was great-great-grandson of Niall of the Nine Hostages, an Irish high king of the 5th century. After studying at the monastic school of Movilla under St Finnian, Columba entered the monastery of Clonard (in County Meath). In early Christian Ireland, druidic traditions collapsed and were replaced with Christian doctrine.

Columba founded several monasteries, including on Iona, which was part of the Irish kingdom of Dál Riata. On his journey to see Brude, Columba is reported to have saved a swimmer from a 'beast' in the River Ness. He gave the creature the sign of the cross and imprecation: *'Thou shalt go no further, nor touch the man; go back with all speed'*. The beast fled, which some suggest was the first sighting of the 'Loch Ness Monster'. Terrified Pict onlookers were amazed and soon glorified Columba's God.

After setting up a church near Invermoriston, Columba performed many apparent miracles. Known as *Clachan Cholumchille* (Columba's Church), the site was near a well. Until his visit, the well water was considered poisonous. Locals feared the toxic water as it caused boils if touched and even death if drunk. Columba blessed the well and, allegedly, drove out evil spirits from its depths. The water at once turned pure and was considered remarkable for its curative properties. In his ever-quest to turn the Pict populace godly, Columba used the well to baptise local pagans who had converted to Christianity. Columba never did convert King Brude, but his saintly miracles legacy lives on.

Address Invermoriston, Inverness, IV63 7YA | **Getting there** Signed archway opposite Invermoriston Falls car park – descend steps to a platform above the well; Citylink Bus 919, stop at Invermoriston, then a short walk | **Hours** Unrestricted, but best seen during daylight | **Tip** Visit Corrimony Chambered Cairn, a near-complete ancient burial monument dating from 2000 B.C. (in Glen Urquhart, west of Drumnadrochit off A831, IV63 6TW).

46 The Unfinished Memorial

Burial site of the last hereditary piper

Renowned for its rugged landscapes, picturesque villages and medieval castles, the Isle of Skye is an indented coastline of peninsulas and narrow lochs, radiating from a mountainous interior. The place is blessed with stories of intrigue and mystery. One such story can be found in Kilmuir Graveyard. A large gravestone lies flat on the ground, almost as if the mason had absconded during engraving the epitaph. The incomplete inscription reads: 'Here lies the remains of Charles MacKarter whose fame as an honest man and remarkable piper will survive this generation for his manners were easy and regular as his music and the the melody of his fingers will' – with an unfinished sentence, the remaining half of the headstone is blank.

This is the burial spot of Charles MacArthur, the last hereditary piper to clan chief MacDonald who lived in Duntulm Castle. It is believed that the headstone had been commissioned by Charles' son, Donald. However, when Donald accidentally drowned in The Minch, a strait that separates the mainland from the Hebridean chain, the mason stopped work, knowing he would not get paid. Of course, another reason might be the fact that the incompetent mason had spelt MacArthur incorrectly as 'MacKarter' or that he had wrongly inscribed 'the the' twice. Either way, there is no record of what the full declaration would have been.

A memorial cairn to the famous MacArthur pipers is found near Duntulm Castle. Historically, a piper always marched in front of an army, playing his troops into battle. Bagpipes were commonly used during clan battles and fights against the English. They signalled orders and tactical manoeuvres, as well as firing of weapons. Not only soldiers, the pipers were also morale boosters, who celebrated victories while mourning the fallen. Unarmed, as they could not carry bagpipes and a weapon, pipers had a very high death rate.

Address Kilmuir Graveyard, Portree, Isle of Skye, IV51 9UE | **Getting there** Car parking at the nearby Skye Museum of Island Life; follow gravel path from the museum to the cemetery – some steps and uneven ground | **Hours** Unrestricted | **Tip** Visit the *Hercules the Bear* sculpture, a memorial to a performing brown bear whose showbiz escape during the 1980s caused a sensation on the Outer Hebrides (off the A867, North Uist, HS6 5HA).

47 Well of the Seven Heads

Beheaded murderers and Highland clan justice

A needle-like obelisk with a macabre tale stands by the side of Loch Oich. Erected in 1812 by the chief of Clan MacDonald, the monument marks an ancient well and recalls gruesome Highland justice. The Well of the Seven Heads is a saga of internal strife where inter-clan hostility was commonplace in the 16th and 17th centuries. It also shows the overwhelming sense of vengeance and power masquerading as justice that typified the Highland clan system.

On 25 September 1663, brothers Alexander and Ranald of Keppoch were slain during a violent brawl in the mansion of Insch. The killers were their uncle – Alexander MacDonald – and his six sons from Inverlair. In a place dominated by the MacDonalds, justice for the murders was not forthcoming. Lord MacDonald of Glengarry and Aros, regarded as the high chief of Clan McDonald, refused to get involved. However, Iain Lom – the Gaelic Poet Laureate of Scotland and a relative of the victims – sought revenge for the killings. After lobbying the Privy Council in Edinburgh, Lom was issued with letters of 'Fire and Sword'. This meant that Lom would not be prosecuted for the summary execution of the murderers. With a posse of 50 men, Lom travelled to Inverlair and the MacDonalds' home and brutally avenged the murder of the Keppoch brothers. The seven known killers were all beheaded.

To prove his retribution to Lord MacDonald, Lom wrapped the severed heads in his plaid. To make the heads more presentable to MacDonald, Lom washed them in the Loch well where the monument now stands. Afterwards, the heads were sent to Edinburgh and affixed to gallows. The bodies of the seven were buried in a mound near Inverlair. A later exhumation of the grave revealed seven headless corpses. Iain Lom had got his bloody vengeance after all. So, cast a glance at the waters of Loch Oich and it might just turn a curious shade of (blood) red.

Address By Spean Bridge, PH34 4EB | Getting there Well is found on south-bound A 82 (busy fast-moving traffic) 1.5 miles south of Invergarry, opposite Well of Seven Heads coffee shop; buses 510B, 915, 916 and 919 stop close by | Hours Unrestricted | Tip Visit the Last Clansman Memorial, where James Stewart was left hanging for four years after a miscarriage of justice following the 1752 Appin Murder (south of Ballachulish Bridge, Ballachulish, PH49 4JX).

48 Willie MacRae Memorial

A mysterious death and tales of foul play

Willie MacRae (1923–1985) was a Scottish lawyer, academic, politician and prominent anti-nuclear campaigner. He was an officer in the Royal Navy and an aide to Lord Mountbatten, who was murdered by the IRA in 1979. MacRae was also a Professor at the University of Haifa in Israel. MacRae was fiercely opposed to storing nuclear weapons in Scotland and a keen campaigner for Scottish independence. On 6 April 1985, MacRae was found slumped in his crashed car overlooking Loch Loyne by two Australian tourists. With a gunshot wound above his right ear, he later died in hospital without regaining consciousness. The verdict was suicide. Israel planted 3,000 trees in his memory.

However, his death has left a lasting controversy. A gun without MacRae's fingerprints was discovered 60 feet from the car, with two spent cartridges and five remaining rounds. The police also kept no record of the precise location of the car. At the time of his death, MacRae was working to counter plans to dump nuclear waste into the sea from Dounreay power station. His house had been burgled several times and one of his friends had recently died in an unexplained house fire. MacRae took to carrying his Dounreay papers in his briefcase. No briefcase was ever found. A copy of his papers was in his office but stolen when it was burgled. No other items were taken. MacRae's last words to a friend were 'I've got them this time'.

Though people have petitioned for a Fatal Accident Inquiry, no such action has been taken. In 1991, Channel 4 found evidence that MacRae was under surveillance by UK intelligence services. They claimed his death involved 'foul play'. In 1990, the pro-independence *Siol nan Gaidheal* group erected a cairn memorial near the crash site. Fresh controversy arose in 2018 when a nurse who claims to have treated MacRae said the gunshot was to the back of his neck, not his temple.

Address Willie MacRae Memorial Cairn, off the A87, near Bun Loyne, Greenfield, Invergarry, PH35 4HR | Getting there The cairn is found near the roadside on the A87 overlooking Loch Loyne; no car parking but places to stop with care | Hours Unrestricted | Tip Visit Ralston Cairn, a lonely memorial to 32-year-old local train driver Ralston Claud Muir who died of leukaemia in 2000 (off the A82, The Meeting of Three Waters, near Glencoe, PH49 4HX, hike north-east into the hills, about 380 yards up from roadside).

49 Ailie's Cairn

Cruel misogynistic murder from yesteryear

At the edge of Holyrood Park, a cluster of rocks bursting out of the earth looks like a quirk of geology. Locals and tourists often pass by without realising its significance. However, in Edinburgh where statues and plaques abound, this strange pile of rocks is a traditional Scottish 'cairn' – a marker in the landscape – to remember a cruel murder.

Known locally as 'Muschat's Cairn', the rockery marks where Nichol Muschat murdered his wife Ailie on 17 October 1720. The tragic story is one of domestic abuse and misogyny. Muschat, a local surgeon, had wooed Ailie in a courtship that lasted three weeks before they were married. He quickly tired of married life and planned her demise. Muschat paid Mr Campbell of Burnbank 20 guineas to kill Ailie, but he failed. He then planned to divorce Ailie by destroying her character. Muschat entered a conspiracy with Campbell, whom he set up to sexually assault Ailie, thereby accusing her of adultery. Campbell backed out of the plot. Undeterred, Muschat with his brother James, and his wife, planned to poison Ailie. That attempt also failed. So, Muschat while on a walk with Ailie in Holyrood Park, cut her throat and abandoned her body to the cold autumn night. She was just 17 years old.

Muschat confessed the killing to his brother, whereupon James demanded money to commit perjury. Under arrest, Muschat simply said he had 'grown weary' of his wife. He was hanged in the Grassmarket in January 1721 and Campbell was transported to Australia. James Muschat and his wife were not charged, for lack of evidence. Today, where misogyny and domestic abuse continues, as well as a patriarchy of remembrance, this tragedy is a warning from history. Violence against women is long lived in culture. That our forebears objected to it and memorialised it should teach us all. The cairn may have Nichol Muschat's name, but this is not just his story!

Address Duke's Walk, Edinburgh, EH8 7AT | **Getting there** Cairn is at the northern end of Holyrood Park; check website for regular road closures, parking and local transport: www.historicenvironment.scot/visit-a-place/places/holyrood-park | **Hours** Unrestricted | **Tip** See the 'Sanctuary Stones', three stones inscribed with a copper 'S' demarcating a refuge for those pursued by debt collectors in the 1800s (junction of Abbey Strand and Horse Wynd, Edinburgh, EH8 8DU).

50 Barnton Nuclear Bunker

Declassified but still hidden

Hidden beneath Corstorphine Hill, the same hill where Edinburgh Zoo is located, is Scotland's biggest and deepest Cold War bunker. Unknown to most people for decades, Barnton Nuclear Bunker was built in 1944 and expanded in 1951. It had been used as an RAF Fighter Command Centre during World War II. However, with advancements in radar technology, the site became redundant by 1955. In 1952, a three-level bunker was added as a Sector Operations Centre (SOC). In 1960, Barnton became a protected control centre in case of a Soviet nuclear attack.

With the Cold War (1947–1991) based on ideological and geopolitical struggles for global domination between the USA and the former USSR, Barnton was a first line of defence for Armageddon. The government believed Barnton would have been able to withstand a 3MT nuclear denotation on Edinburgh city centre. According to the CND (Campaign for Nuclear Disarmament) in the early 1980s, up to 90 per cent of Edinburgh's populace would have been killed or maimed during such a nuclear attack. During the height of the Cold War, over 200 military installations and bases were housed in Scotland. Today, submarines with the UK's nuclear deterrent remain based at HMNB Clyde, a 30-minute drive from Glasgow.

Barnton closed in 1983, and Lothian Council took ownership. The site was intended for housing, but this never materialised. Purchased for £60,000 in 1996 by James Mitchell, and despite suffering vandalism and a major fire in 1998, the bunker is undergoing a restoration programme. The site aims to be a visitor attraction and museum of Cold War Heritage. Barnton Bunker spans a significant period of the 20th century and is the only remaining well-preserved three-level bunker in Britain. It is a unique example of how an emergency government would work from an underground hub, trying to ensure survival and recovery in a post-apocalyptic world.

Address 35 Clermiston Road, Edinburgh, EH4 7BN, www.barntonbunker.com | Getting there Buses 21 and 200 Skylink to Clermiston Road North; small car park nearby, then a short walk – located up the hill behind metal railings | Hours Sat 1pm, via dedicated tours (see www.barntonbunker.com/book-your-tour) | Tip Follow *6 Times*, a succession of six eerily emerging sculptural iron figures by Antony Gormley that lead from Edinburgh's city centre hauntingly into the sea (start at Figure 1, The Modern Art Gallery, Edinburgh, EH4 3DR).

51 Battle of Pinkie Cleugh

First modern battle on British soil

On 10 September 1547 near the River Esk at Musselburgh, the Battle of Pinkie Cleugh was the final and biggest pitched battle to be fought between English and Scottish armies. As a defining conflict for Anglo-Scots relations, it was also considered to be the first modern battle on British soil, with traditional weapons of bows and arrows being used alongside firearms and naval bombardments.

King Henry VIII of England tried to secure an alliance with Scotland by the marriage of infant Mary, Queen of Scots, to his child son, the future Edward VI. Scotland rejected the idea, partly because of fears of religious Reformation on English terms. Henry looked to change Scottish minds by force – what became known as the 'Rough Wooing'. However, Henry died in 1547, and the Duke of Somerset, uncle to Edward VI, became Lord Protector. Somerset continued with the 'Rough Wooing' policy and gathered an 18,000-man army at Berwick. Supported by a fleet of 30 warships, the English moved towards Edinburgh. Scottish defences were led by the Earl of Arran who mustered a 22,000-man army. Blocking Somerset's advance on the Scottish capital, the English charged. Scottish resistance crumbled and the slaughter was intense. The English chased remnants of the Scottish army over a significant area and butchered those retreating. Over 15,000 men died. The Scottish defeat is known as 'Black Saturday'.

This was a battle of a (Scottish) medieval army against an (English) renaissance army. With innovations in naval warfare and weaponry, conflicts became ever bloodier. A year later, the Siege of Haddington (1548–49) brought the War of Rough Wooing to an end. As for the courtship or 'wooing', Queen Mary was smuggled out of Scotland to France, as part of the 'Auld Alliance' between Scotland and France. She later married 14-year-old Francis, Dauphin of France in 1558. She was 15 years old.

Address Battle of Pinkie Cleugh Memorial Stone, Eskfield Cottages, Wallyford, Musselburgh, EH21 8BH | **Getting there** Located as part of a Battlefield Heritage Trail; the memorial is found off the A 1 (A 6094 junction); buses 44, 111, 111A, 112, X6 and X44 to St Clements Well | **Hours** Unrestricted | **Tip** See the 'Rough Wooing' Memorial, sculptures depicting Scottish and English soldiers in combat during the Battle of Pinkie Cleugh (23 Clark Avenue, Musselburgh, EH21 7BS).

52 The Black Mausoleum

Where the 'bluidy' ghost of George MacKenzie roams

Within Greyfriars Kirkyard is the final resting place of Sir George MacKenzie (1636–1691). The MacKenzie Mausoleum – or the 'Black Mausoleum' – takes the form of a large rotunda, divided into eight bays. Small windows called 'lucarnes' pierce the stone roof to illuminate the interior. The lintel above the entrance is decorated with emblems signifying death and mortality.

MacKenzie was a lawyer and Lord Advocate and a man of literary tendencies. He published many legal, political and antiquarian books, including *Aretina* in 1660, the first Scottish novel. He also contributed to witchcraft trials in 1661 and defended the 'witch' Maevia. Ironically, MacKenzie attributed witch confessions to the use of torture. His *Laws and Customs of Scotland in Matters Criminal* (1678) was the first textbook of Scottish criminal law, in which MacKenzie defended judicial torture. It was for brutal torture that 'Bluidy (Bloody) MacKenzie' became infamous.

Responsible for the persecuting policy of King Charles II against Presbyterian Covenanters, who railed against royal authority, MacKenzie enthusiastically meted out public torture and extrajudicial executions. He was responsible for up to 18,000 Covenanters' deaths, known as the Killing Times (1679–1688). Proud of his callous accomplishments, MacKenzie had his tomb at Greyfriars, the site of his many merciless deeds. Today, reports of the MacKenzie Poltergeist abound, with tales of hauntings and malevolent forces. His supposed restless spirit has reportedly caused supernatural bruising and scratches on mausoleum visitors. When a schoolchild from George Heriot's hid in the tomb to escape a beating from a master, he supposedly got trapped and lost his mind when confronted by a ghost. Generations of local children have taunted the 'ghost' with the rhyme: 'Bluidy MacKenzie, come oot if ye daur! Lift the sneck and draw the bar!'

Address Greyfriars Kirk, Greyfriars Place, Edinburgh, EH1 2QQ, www.greyfriars.com | **Getting there** Buses 9, 23, 27, 35, 41 and 42 all stop close by; train to Edinburgh Waverley station then a 10-minute walk; the mausoleum is in a locked section and can be viewed at a distance | **Hours** Unrestricted for the exterior; access to the interior is via official 'City of the Dead' tours (www.cityofthedeadtours.com) | **Tip** See the Jougs Collar of Duddingston Kirk, a medieval device to punish wrongdoers that still hangs outside a village church (5 Old Church Lane, Duddingston, Edinburgh, EH15 3PX).

53 Burke & Hare Murder Dolls

Mysterious miniature coffins and tiny doll corpses

On 25 June 1836, a group of schoolchildren discovered 17 miniature wooden coffins at Arthur's Seat, the iconic ancient extinct volcano in Edinburgh. Complete with tiny, individual wooden dolls as corpses dressed in burial clothes, no one is sure when, who or what they were made for. Only eight now survive, all of which are shown at the National Museum of Scotland, who had them gifted in 1901.

Theories of the 'Fairy Coffins', as they have been referred to, range from satanic effigies to tributes to sailors lost at sea. However, the most popular explanation is that the coffins stand for the 17 victims of the 'Anatomy Murders' by William Burke and William Hare. With a shortage in the legal supply of fresh cadavers for medical anatomy experiments, Burke and Hare turned to murder. In 1828, over the course of 10 months, they sold corpses to Robert Knox, an anatomist, and Fellow of the Royal Society of Edinburgh. Knox's incautious methods of obtaining cadavers for dissections saw him buying corpses from Burke and Hare for up £10 each (worth over £1,360 today). With a corpse shortage, Burke and Hare began murdering their lodgers (mostly women) after they fell ill or passed out drunk, by smothering them with pillows. Burke and Hare were caught and tried, with Hare giving King's evidence against Burke. A crowd of 25,000 people watched Burke hang, while Hare was never seen again as he headed for the English border after his release from jail.

The discovery of the 17 tiny coffins not long after Burke's execution soon attracted a link with the 17 victims of Burke and Hare. One suggestion is that a Victorian-obsessed follower of the murders created the coffins to mimic the burials that the victims never received. Whatever the origin or reason for the coffins, today they are a way of keeping the memory of Burke and Hare's victims alive.

Address National Museum of Scotland, Chambers Street, Edinburgh, EH1 1JF, +44 (0) 300 123 6789, www.nms.ac.uk/national-museum-of-scotland | Getting there 'Murder Dolls' found in 'Daith Comes In' Gallery, Level 4; buses 35 and 45 to National Museum of Scotland | Hours Daily 10am–5pm, closed Christmas | Tip Keep the memory of Fawziyah Javed alive by visiting her memorial bench. She was pushed off Arthur's Seat in 2021 by her husband, killing her and her unborn child (foot of Arthur's Seat, Queen's Drive, Holyrood Park, Edinburgh, EH8 8HG).

54 Canine Cemetery

Final resting place for doggy companions

Edinburgh Castle looms over the capital city of Scotland. Standing on Castle Rock, the impressive castle was home to King Malcolm III in the 11th century until its royal-residential role declined in the 15th century. By the 17th century, the castle was used principally as a military garrison, though it has been used as a prison, an arsenal, a treasury and mint, as well as a national archive.

Steeped in legends and myths, the Lone Piper and the Ghost of the Headless Drummer are said to haunt the castle. By the 19th century, Edinburgh Castle became a national monument. However, during this period, an obscure and almost hidden graveyard was incorporated into the castle grounds.

In 1837, at the beginning of Queen Victoria's reign, a small garden space at the top of the castle became the final resting place of soldiers' dogs. The canine cemetery is one of only two in Scotland – the other being at Fort George, near Inverness. It has about 20 burial plots for dogs, mostly regimental mascots or from high-ranking officers. Many of the headstones have badly weathered, but the oldest surviving epitaph is a dedication to 'Jess', the band dog of the Black Watch 42nd Royal Highlanders, who died in 1881.

The most recent grave from 1980 commemorates 'Winkle', the 'dear and faithful friend of Lady Gow and the [castle] Governor'. Other dogs buried here include 'Dobbler', who travelled with the Argyll and Sutherland Highlanders to China, Ceylon (Sri Lanka) and South Africa, and 'Tinker', who was General William's dog.

A verse allegedly penned by Scottish poet Robbie Burns notes the cemetery: 'Berkin dugs here lie at rest / The yappin worst, obedient best / Sodgers pets and mascots tae / Still guard the castle to this day'. However, the ode has been mistakenly attributed to the national bard. Instead, Ali Strachan compiled the poem for a Burns Night Supper while working for Historic Environment Scotland.

Address Edinburgh Castle Dog Cemetery, The Esplanade, Edinburgh, EH1 2NG, www.edinburghcastle.scot | Getting there Cemetery is located inside Edinburgh Castle; buses 23, 27 and X52 to Victoria Street then a 10-minute walk; train to Edinburgh Waverley station then a 15-minute walk | Hours The dog cemetery is inaccessible to visitors but can be viewed from above. See website for seasonal opening times. | Tip Visit Mons Meg, an enormous cannon given to King James II as a wedding gift and fired only once in anger against the English at Norham Castle in 1497. Mons Meg is in Edinburgh Castle.

55 Covenanters' Prison

Dying for your religion

Before the 1707 Acts of Union, which merged the kingdoms of England and Scotland into Great Britain, the 1603 Union of the Crowns saw the two countries share a monarch. However, in 1638, dissatisfaction over religion within the state saw the National Covenant signed in Greyfriars Kirkyard. Presbyterian Scots considered Christ to be head of the Church as opposed to the monarch, King Charles I, who thought of himself as 'divinely appointed'. Charles made changes to Scottish religious practices, including introducing an English prayer book into Scottish religious services.

The National Covenant marked a significant stand for Scottish autonomy. It sparked the Bishops' War in 1639, when Charles marched troops into Scotland. After the Wars of the Three Kingdoms (1639–1653), which included the English Civil War, Charles I was executed, but the eventual restoration of the monarchy came with King Charles II. Charles II imposed strict religious conditions, particularly on Presbyterian Covenanters. After Covenanters rebelled in 1679 and lost to Charles II at the Battle of Bothwell Bridge, 1,184 prisoners were brought to Greyfriars. A few prisoners took the 'King's Peace' and pledged allegiance to the Crown.

Prisoners were left in the walled graveyard, which became known as the 'Covenanters' Prison'. Open to the elements for four months, starved prisoners had extreme violence and torture meted out by Sir George 'Bloody' Mackenzie, a Lord Advocate. In November 1679, with many prisoners dead through maltreatment or execution, the remaining 257 men were sent to the colonies. However, the transport ship to America was wrecked off the coast of Orkney, leaving only 48 survivors. A small plaque in Greyfriars Kirkyard commemorates the gruesome experiences of the Covenanters at the hands of those like Mackenzie, who is also buried nearby in the alleged haunted 'Black Mausoleum'.

Address Greyfriars Kirkyard, Greyfriars Place, Edinburgh, EH1 2QQ, www.greyfriars.com | Getting there The Covenanters' Prison Memorial is found at the south-western corner of the kirkyard; buses 9, 23, 27, 35, 41 and 42 all stop close by; train to Edinburgh Waverley station then a 10-minute walk | Hours Unrestricted | Tip Visit the Covenanters' Monument, the site where many Covenanters were hanged, and where a representation of the gallows is made on the ground with different coloured stones (Grassmarket, Edinburgh, EH1 2JU, www.covenanter.org.uk).

56 Craigentinny Marbles

Imposing 'suburban' tomb of an eccentric landowner

An enormous, elaborate tomb looks oddly out of place next to a bowling club. Known as the 'Craigentinny Marbles', this is the mausoleum of William Henry Miller (1789–1848), a wealthy landowner and Member of Parliament for Newcastle-under-Lyme in Staffordshire, England. Having spent little time in Scotland, Miller lost his parliamentary seat in 1841 and retired to his Craigentinny estate, once rural fields but now a suburb of north-east Edinburgh.

Miller was an avid book collector. But he was less interested in books' contents, rather their size. He liked tall books and carried a ruler to measure any book he wished to buy. In London bookshops, he was referred to as 'Measure Miller'. As an eccentric, Miller was unmarried and childless. He died aged 60 on 31 October 1848. According to his will, he instructed that a large mausoleum be built at a cost of £20,000 (£3.75 million today) on his estate and decorated with sculptured friezes. He also wanted to be buried at 40 feet deep, rather than a standard 6-foot-deep grave.

Designed by David Rhind in 1856, two bas-relief sculptures by Alfred Gatley depicting biblical narratives were added to the mausoleum by 1863. The sculptures were likened to the *Elgin Marbles*, a contested collection of Ancient Greek artworks held by the British Museum. *The Scotsman* newspaper at the time of Miller's death reported a monument would be constructed in 'commemoration of the private virtues of the deceased, for, as a public character, he was unknown'. Speculation about the mausoleum's scale includes tales of Miller being a woman and wanting to be buried deep so as to avoid post-mortem scrutiny. Others suggest Miller was afraid of 'body snatchers', people who stole fresh corpses for the anatomists; hence the imposing tomb. Whatever the case, the monument was appointed a listed building in 1970 and is now incongruously surrounded by bungalows.

Address 3 Craigentinny Crescent, Edinburgh, EH7 6QA | Getting there Buses 15, 21, 26 and 45 to Craigentinny Crescent | Hours Unrestricted | Tip See the statue of John Rattray, the man who helped set up the first rules of golf in 1744 (4 Links Gardens, Leith, Edinburgh, EH6 7JG).

57 Cramond Island

'Ghost island' and former wartime coastal defence

Cramond Island is one of 17 tidal islands in Scotland (and 43 in the UK) that can be walked to from the mainland. Lying a mile out to sea in the Firth of Forth, it is connected across the Drum Sands by a paved causeway. Along the causeway is a row of Brutalist-style concrete pylons that resemble huge teeth. Built as an anti-boat barrier during World War II, the pylons are a reminder that the island was a strategic wartime fortification.

Several islands in the Firth of Forth created a 'Middle Line' of defences to protect anchorage for warships. The defences prevented enemy sea raids on Royal Naval Dockyard Rosyth. Remnants of World War II-era fortifications still survive on Cramond Island and have become a destination for urban exploration (as well as graffiti). Gun emplacements, searchlight buildings and other abandoned military structures litter the island. Close to Cramond Island is Inchmickery, a tiny islet that was also used as a wartime fortification. Inchmickery is inaccessible and a protected wildlife site. The concrete fortified buildings make the islet look like, from a distance at least, a battleship.

Earlier history suggests Cramond Island as the place of Urbs Iudeu, a medieval island fortress from the Dark Ages. Although the site has not been found, according to the 9th-century *Historia Brittonum* as well as the Venerable Bede's *Ecclesiastical History of the English People* (written about A.D. 731), Urbs Iudeu was besieged in A.D. 655 in the war between King Osweo of Northumbria and King Penda of Mercia and located somewhere on the Firth of Forth. While archaeological evidence is lacking for this claim, Cramond Island was the site of a mortal fight in 1596. Authorised by King James IV, the duel on the island between Adam Bruntfield and James Carmichael, judged by the Duke of Lennox, saw Bruntfield kill Carmichael after a quarrel about treason.

Address Cramond, Edinburgh, EH4 6NU | Getting there Bus 41 on Princess Street | Hours Unrestricted, but only accessible during low tides – check nearby noticeboard, or www.tideschart.com or text CRAMOND to 81400, and make sure you leave enough time to return along the causeway before the tide closes over it | Tip Visit the Óscar Romero Plaque, in memory of a human-rights activist and Salvadoran archbishop who was assassinated in 1980 (junction of Dalkeith Road and Romero Place, Edinburgh, EH16 5AE).

58 Death Cell Door

An entrance to execution

Where the Scottish Government's HQ now stands at St Andrew's House on Calton Hill, the infamous Calton Gaol (Jail) once stood. Before Calton was built in 1817, the site was home to the equally notorious Bridewell – Edinburgh's first dedicated prison in 1795. Calton housed some of the worst criminals in Scotland, including the infamous 'body-snatchers' Burke and Hare, imprisoned there in 1828.

Resembling a foreboding medieval castle, and being close to Waverley railway station, some early tourists to Edinburgh mistook the gaol for Edinburgh Castle. Many of the prisoners were indebted women who were too poor to pay the bond to escape incarceration. But the prison was also a place of execution, usually by hanging. Condemned prisoners had been executed at Calton Hill for centuries, with a gibbet erected in 1554. Many of the prisoners were buried in unconsecrated graves within the prison grounds. Today, 10 of these graves still lie hidden beneath the car park at St Andrew's House. Executed prisoners were buried head-first with their feet facing the sky, as no church would accept bodies of the condemned. Part of the death cell where the condemned were housed before their hanging is still accessible at St Andrew's House.

Calton was demolished in 1930; its rubble used for building the Hopes Reservoir Dam in the Lammermuir Hills. Yet, the imposing wooden door to the death cell survived and found its way to the Beehive Inn, a former 16th-century coaching house in the Grassmarket. The door would have been the last entrance walked through by fated convicts. These included Eugène Chantrelle, hanged in 1878 for poisoning his wife; Jessie 'Baby Farmer' King, the last woman to be executed in 1889, for murdering children in her care; Patrick Higgins, who killed his two sons in 1913; and Philip Murray, the last person to be hanged in 1923, for killing his wife's lover.

Address Beehive Inn, 18–20 Grassmarket, Edinburgh, EH1 2JU, +44 (0) 131 225 7171, www.belhaven.co.uk/pubs/midlothian/beehive-inn | Getting there The 'death door' is found on the second landing accessible by stairs, located across from the main entrance – check with staff first if you are not a customer of the Beehive Inn | Hours Sun–Thu noon–midnight, Fri & Sat noon–1am | Tip Visit The Edinburgh Dungeon and discover Edinburgh's darkest history through re-enactments, theatrical sets and rides (31 Market Place, Edinburgh, EH1 1DF, www.thedungeons.com/edinburgh).

59 Dechmont UFO Monument

The only UK criminal case for an alien encounter

On 9 November 1979, forestry worker Robert Taylor reported an alien spaceship in Dechmont Woods. Known as the 'Dechmont Woods Encounter', the spot where the alleged extraterrestrial rendezvous took place is now part of a scenic walking trail. Apparently, Taylor chanced upon a UFO (Unidentified Flying Object) hovering above the forest floor. With a strong acrid smell, the dome-like craft dispatched two smaller spheres that dragged Taylor up to the larger machine. He reported being grabbed and pulled up by his legs. After passing out, he recovered and returned home with torn clothes and cuts to his body.

Taylor reported the episode as an assault to the police, and the incident is the only UFO sighting in the UK to be classified as a criminal investigation. Police discovered a series of deep, regular marks on the ground where the UFO had been. The unusual pattern included 32 holes, each with a 3.5-inch diameter. These resembled ladder marks, and police could not match them to any machinery held by the Forestry Commission. Crime forensics said rips in Taylor's trousers seemed to have been made by something hooking them and dragging him upwards. The case made worldwide headlines at the time.

Whether this was a UFO or not is open to speculation. Other explanations have included everything from hallucinatory berries to ball lightning, or even a mirage of the planet Venus. A medical reason could lie in Taylor having an epileptic seizure, but there is no evidence of this. While the event has passed into legend, Taylor, who was a war hero, never changed his story and died in 2007. No one doubts that Taylor genuinely believed what he saw was real. The issue is that the UFO has never made a reappearance. In 2023, the US Pentagon opened an online reporting tool for unidentified anomalous phenomena, formerly known as UFOs.

Address Dechmont Law and UFO Trail, Eastwood Park, Deans, Livingston, EH54 8PS | **Getting there** Car parking on Eastwood Park – boulder and plaque mark the 'UFO incident' site; buses X25, X28 and 280 to Deans Community High School; train to Livingston North station then a 15-minute walk | **Hours** Unrestricted, but unadvisable to visit during hours of darkness | **Tip** See the Almondell Wallacestone, an unassuming stone that is the oldest Scottish memorial to William Wallace, dated 1784 (Almondell Country Park, Broxburn East Entrance, Broxburn, EH52 5PE).

60 Dolly the Sheep

A cloned mammal that pushed ethical envelopes

Dolly the Sheep was the first cloned animal created from an adult cell. While not the first large mammal to be cloned, Dolly broke scientific ground by being cloned from a single mammary cell that held all the DNA information to create a whole new sheep. Dolly was born on 5 July 1996 at Edinburgh University's Roslin Institute. Named after Dolly Parton, the American country singer, Dolly the Sheep started life as a single cell in a test tube. The nucleus was extracted from a Finn Dorset sheep and placed into an empty egg cell from a Scottish Blackface sheep and then transferred into a surrogate mother.

Her birth sparked both excitement and ethical debate about cloning. The media frenzy that followed made an irresistible leap from cloned animal livestock to cloned humans. In June 1997, President Clinton instructed the US Congress to pass a human-cloning ban. Dolly also raised moral debates about controversial embryonic stem cells. As with cloning, the aim of stem cell research was to develop therapies for human disease using genetic engineering. Harvested from aborted embryos, stem cells could be combined with cloning technology to clone people. President George W. Bush severely restricted embryonic stem cell research in 2001.

As a result, armies of 'designer babies' never occurred, though livestock cloning is used for agricultural breeding. In the UK, it is illegal to sell cloned animals for food. Meanwhile, Dolly gave birth to six lambs, with help from a Welsh Mountain ram called David. Dolly only lived until she was six years old and was euthanised after she developed arthritis and lung cancer caused by Jaagsiekte sheep retrovirus (JSRV). The average age for a sheep is 10–12 years. Her taxidermised body was donated to the National Museum of Scotland as an exhibit. Dolly continues to create ethical dialogue about genetics, biology and reproductive technologies.

Address National Museum of Scotland (Science & Technology Gallery), Chambers Street, Edinburgh, EH1 1JF, +44 (0) 300 123 6789, www.nms.ac.uk | Getting there Buses 1, 10, 11, 15 and 16 to Chambers Street; train to Edinburgh Waverley station then a 15-minute walk | Hours Daily 10am–5pm, closed Christmas | Tip Visit remnants of The Flodden Wall, built in 1560 to protect Edinburgh from an English invasion that never came (1 Vennel, Edinburgh, EH1 2HU or 26 Pleasance, Edinburgh, EH8 9RW).

61 Dr Dewar Monument

Remembering a killer physician

Edinburgh is full of monuments dedicated to famous dead men. But one has a much darker story and has been forgotten – until now! In a small park in the quaint seaside suburb of Portobello, a memorial fountain is inscribed with: 'This fountain has been erected in remembrance of Dr Hugh Dewar, Portobello, by his grateful patients and numerous friends, who deplore the loss in the prime of manhood of a kind friend and skilful and beloved physician. His quiet charity was known to the needy. 1866–1914'.

Despite a glowing epitaph, on 4 February 1914, pregnant Jane Anderson visited Dewar to have her baby delivered. Working from his surgery on Brighton Street, this should have been a routine operation for the well-respected and experienced doctor. However, Jane underwent an excruciating labour, where Dewar noticed a protruding 'tube' from Jane. Thinking it was the umbilical cord, Dewar pulled out the four-and-a-half-meter mucous membrane lining of her large intestine. For a qualified doctor, the appalling mistake was incomprehensible. Jane died in agony, aged 25. Her baby also died.

Three weeks later, Dewar was charged with culpable homicide but was still allowed to practise. As well as a criminal charge, Jane's police constable husband – Duncan Anderson – brought a civil case against Dewar, citing professional negligence. On his trial day, Dewar took ill and later died the same day. Without an official autopsy, his death certificate cites 'narcotic poison' as the reason for his demise. His cause of death was not made public at the time.

Despite his suicide and evasion of justice, a fund of £310 7s 4d was raised for Dewar's memorial. Jane is buried in Portobello Cemetery, with no ornate headstone. Dewar's most memorable act was killing a young woman in childbirth by his medical incompetence, then cheating justice. Today, the question is – where is Jane's fountain?

Address Abercorn Park, Pittville Street, Portobello, Edinburgh, EH15 2BZ | Getting there Buses 19 and 26 to Pittville Street; train to Brunstane station then a 20-minute walk | Hours Unrestricted | Tip Visit the Dr Balfour memorial, a more uplifting story where Balfour treated trapped miners in 1884 and worked tirelessly during an 1890 influenza epidemic (junction of Klondyke Street & Newcraighall Road, Musselburgh, EH21 8SQ).

62 The Edinburgh Maiden

A beheading machine that executed its inventor

Many associate the guillotine with executions of 'Reign of Terror' during the French Revolution. The 'clean-death' machine is often attributed to Joseph-Ignace Guillotin in 1792. Yet, a guillotine predecessor was first used 400 years earlier in Halifax, England. The Halifax Gibbet decapitated over 100 convicts from 1286 to 1650 and became the inspiration for a 'beheading machine' in Edinburgh. The 'Maiden' as it became known, was the only one of its kind in Scotland. It was used in 150 public executions from 1564 to 1710.

The 'Maiden' is thought to have been the idea of James Douglas, Fourth Earl of Morton. Impressed by the 'clean work' of the Halifax Gibbet, Douglas proposed a similar means of execution. In 1564, carpenters Adam and Patrick Schang and George Tod built the 'Maiden' out of oak with a lead weight and iron blade. Constructed as a portable machine, a kind of flat-pack killing device, it was reassembled and executed convicts in and around Edinburgh. The convict would place his/her head on a crossbar about four feet from the bottom, a position known as 'kissing the Maiden'. Within its frame, a peg would keep the blade in place. Removing the peg saw the blade fall and behead the condemned in an instant.

The first to 'kiss the Maiden' was Thomas Scott of Cambusmichael on 3 April 1565. Other notable victims include Archibald Campbell, First Marquess of Argyll in 1661, beheaded for high treason following the restoration of King Charles II. In 1685, his son, the Ninth Earl of Argyll, was also executed for rebellion against King James VII.

For his complicity in the murder of Lord Darney – husband of Mary, Queen of Scots – in 1567, James Douglas was executed by the 'Maiden'. Ironically, the inventor of the 'Maiden' met his grisly end on the contraption he designed. The original 'Maiden' is now on display at the National Museum of Scotland.

Address National Museum of Scotland, Chambers Street, Edinburgh, EH1 1JF, +44 (0) 300 123 6789, www.nms.ac.uk | Getting there The 'Maiden' is displayed in the Kingdom of Scots exhibition (Level 1); buses 35 and 45 to Chambers Street | Hours Daily 10am–5pm, closed Christmas | Tip In the same exhibition, discover other items of capital punishment and torture from the Middle Ages, including thumbscrews, stocks and a scold's bridle.

63_'Great Lafayette' Grave

Magical life and curious death

Sigmund Neuberger, born in Munich in 1871, was one of the most celebrated illusionists of his time. After emigrating to the USA, he performed in the theatrical genre of vaudeville. Adopting the stage name of 'The Great Lafayette', and with vaudeville evolving from comedy acts to serious magic shows, eccentric and ill-tempered Neuberger fared very well. With a weekly wage of £350 (over £51,000 today), Neuberger included Harry Houdini among his few friends.

Houdini gifted Neuberger a terrier dog, named Beauty. The dog became the soulmate of Neuberger, who indulged the canine with diamond-encrusted collars and rich meals. Beauty died on 5 May 1911 of apoplexy, caused by over-feeding, during a season at the Empire Theatre in Edinburgh. Grief-stricken Neuberger had Beauty embalmed and buried at Piershill Cemetery, on condition of him also being buried in the same grave at his passing.

Tragically, that burial took place a few days later, when Neuberger was killed in a theatre fire. With 3,000 spectators packing the Empire Theatre on 9 May, Neuberger's act was one of remarkable illusions and elaborate scenarios. His finale was the 'Lion's Bride' whereby Neuberger would magically change places with a lion inside a cage. As 'The Great Lafayette' took his final bow, a lantern fell and set fire to the stage scenery. The audience, thinking it was part of the show, were slow to be evacuated. With the stage ablaze, hampered by locked doors that Neuberger had ordered to stop people stealing his tricks, 11 people were killed. Included in the dead was the lion and a 15-year-old dwarf called Alice Dale who operated a mechanical teddy bear. A body thought to be that of Neuberger was in fact the corpse of his body double. Neuberger was found later and identified by diamond rings on his fingers. Today, the theatre is said to be haunted by the roar of a lion.

Address Piershill Cemetery, 204 Piersfield Place, Edinburgh, EH8 7BN | **Getting there** Buses 15, 26 and 45 to Piershill Cemetery | **Hours** Unrestricted | **Tip** Visit an apparent healing site for pilgrims with eye ailments where St Triduana allegedly plucked out her eyeballs and gave them to King Nectan (Shrine of St Triduana, 29 Restalrig Road South, Edinburgh, EH7 6LF).

64 Greyfriars Kirkyard

'Non Omnis Moriar' (Not All of Me Will Die)

Located on the southern edge of Edinburgh's Old Town is Greyfriars Kirkyard, once a Franciscan friary where friars wore grey habits – hence 'Greyfriars' – and the term 'kirk' from Old Norse '*kirkja*' meaning 'church'. Greyfriars has played a symbolic role in the bloody history of Scotland. Following the Scottish Reformation of 1560, the Franciscan monastery passed into the possession of Mary, Queen of Scots. Used as a burial ground, a new church opened in 1620, and a second church in 1722. In the 1930s, both churches were joined.

Greyfriars saw the signing of the National Covenant on 28 February 1638. It was a crucial document in a turbulent period of religious and civil change. The Covenant declared the rights of ordinary people and set the foundations for democratic rule. During 'The Killing Time' (1661–88), an era of conflict between the Presbyterian Covenanter movement and government forces, hundreds of Covenanter prisoners were incarcerated in the Kirkyard. The name 'Covenanters' Prison' stuck and is where most of the enclosed burial lairs are found. A 'Martyr's Monument' commemorates executed Covenanters. Today, 'City of the Dead' tours offer visitors glimpses into the prison, which combine history, humour and horror. Greyfriars Kirkyard is reported to be one of the most haunted graveyards in the world.

Among the many tombstones, the grave of Greyfriars Bobby is the most unusual. Bobby was a terrier dog who stood vigil at his owner's grave for 14 years. His loyalty became legendary. When Bobby died in January 1872, he was laid to rest not far from his master's grave. A statue was erected in 1873 and is Edinburgh's smallest monument. Yet, the story of this loyal canine might be a Victorian publicity stunt. James Brown, caretaker of the cemetery at the time, is believed to have cultivated the myth because it brought in curious visitors – and tips.

Address Greyfriars Kirk, Greyfriars Place, Edinburgh, EH1 2QQ, www.greyfriars.com | Getting there Buses 9, 23, 27, 35, 41 and 42 all stop close by; train to Edinburgh Waverley station then a 10-minute walk | Hours Unrestricted | Tip Follow in the footsteps of Charles Dickens to Canongate Kirkyard, the final resting place of Ebenezer Lennox Scroggie who inspired the character Ebenezer Scrooge (Canongate Kirkyard, 153 Canongate, Edinburgh, EH8 8BN, www.canongatekirk.org.uk).

65 Greyfriars' Mortsafes

Guarding graves against 'resurrectionists'

With views of George Heriot's School – inspiration for the fictional Hogwarts School of Harry Potter fame – Greyfriars Kirkyard is home to several mortsafes. Constructed of heavy metal bars padlocked together, or great stone slabs, early 19th-century mortsafes protected graves from macabre 'body-snatchers'. When anatomy was in its infancy, medical schools required fresh cadavers to experiment on. Only executed convicts were legally available. After a 1505 local charter, anatomists in Edinburgh were given one condemned person a year for the purpose of dissection.

With limited supply, 'resurrectionists' – men who dug up graves and stole bodies – would sell corpses to anatomists. Publicity of the gruesome murders in 1828 by Burke and Hare, who killed 17 people especially for supplying cadavers, raised fears of body snatching. Authorities often ignored the heinous practice, as medical knowledge was being advanced. However, grave-robbing became such a concern that mourners took great pains to protect their deceased. Belief in resurrection of the dead, where the dead are raised for an eternal afterlife, is preached by many religions. It was believed (and still is) that the dead cannot rise in an incomplete state.

So, to guard against any mortal theft and to safeguard a resurrection, 'mortsafes' were invented around 1816. Societies were formed to buy and control the use of mortsafes. Watchtowers were built in many Scottish cemeteries, with people employed as 'watchers' for any 'resurrectionist'. Many churches hired mortsafes out, including for children's graves. Not even the child dead were safe! Mortsafes were placed over graves for about six weeks. They were then removed for further use when the body was sufficiently decayed. The 1882 Anatomy Act effectively put an end to grave robbing and the need for mortsafes, allowing anatomists to obtain cadavers legally.

Address Greyfriars Kirkyard, Edinburgh, EH1 2QE, www.greyfriarskirk.com | Getting there Mortsafes are close to the main cemetery entrance; buses 9, 23, 27, 35, 41 and 42; train to Edinburgh Waverley station then a 10-minute walk | Hours Unrestricted, but best to visit during daylight hours | Tip While in Greyfriars Kirkyard, visit the grave of Thomas Riddell Esq (1734–1806), the real-life inspiration for J. K. Rowling and her supernatural villain Tom Riddle aka Voldemort in the Harry Potter stories.

66 The Hanging Stanes

Last public execution for highway robbery

Embedded into a residential street are two stone bases that recall a dark past. Easy to miss, each base monument in Braid Road is a metre square and surrounded by paving setts. They each have a central socket place, into which gallows would have been erected. This was the spot of the last public execution for highway robbery in Scotland.

In November 1814, Irish labourers Thomas Kelly and Henry O'Neil pistol-whipped David Loch and robbed him of his horse and money. Coupled with anti-Irish sentiment at the time, as well as Kelly and O'Neil having a criminal history, a trial took place in January 1815. With probable racism and bigotry from locals, the jury took no time in deliberation and passed a guilty verdict instantaneously. Rather than being hanged at the Tolbooth, like normal criminals, the judge demanded Kelly and O'Neil be executed at the very spot where the crime occurred. The convicts were chained and marched three miles in a snowstorm to the new gibbet in Braid Road.

Despite the wintery weather, the macabre spectacle attracted a large ghoulish crowd. With city officials dressed in finest regalia, as well as a Catholic priest and Church of Scotland clergy, a veritable procession went with the highwaymen to their fate. Still in their chains, Kelly and O'Neil were hanged and their corpses left hanging at the spot for several years. A barbaric deterrent for others as well as punitive punishment for the crimes committed. Robert Louis Stevenson, a famous Scottish author, visited the Hanging Stanes as a child. He later wrote in 1879 of 'a crow-haunted gibbet, with two bodies hanged in chains'. The last public execution in Edinburgh was George Bryce – the Ratho Murderer – in 1864. Bryce suffered a horrendous death after the hangman botched the public hanging. Executions waned during the later 1800s, with convicts sent to the colonies instead.

Address Near 66 Braid Road, Morningside, Edinburgh, EH10 6AL | Getting there Buses 5, 11, 15 and 16 to Comiston Gardens; train to Slateford station then a 40-minute walk | Hours Unrestricted | Tip Visit the execution spot of George Bryce, the last-ever public hanging in Edinburgh in 1864 (George Bryce Wall Plaque, 17 Lawnmarket (Royal Mile), Edinburgh, EH1 2NX).

67 Heave Awa Hoose

'Dig away chaps, I'm not dead yet'

As Edinburgh's populace grew during the 1800s and was confined by the medieval burgh wall, the city expanded vertically. Building multi-storey tenements saw skyscrapers of the day. However, with no building codes, the Old Town of Edinburgh was hugely overcrowded and harboured harrowing living conditions. Many tall buildings collapsed or were engulfed by flames.

On 24 November 1861 at 1.10am, a 250-year-old, seven-storey tenement succumbed to such a disaster. As 77 inhabitants slept, the dilapidated medieval building collapsed, killing 35 people. Anguished screams of those trapped saw rescuers work through the night to recover bodies and the injured. At dawn, a foot was seen protruding from the debris. It belonged to 12-year-old Joseph McIvor, who had fallen four floors, and miraculously survived. His spirited voice called out to those who were frantically digging him out of the rubble... 'Heave awa' lads, ah'm no deid yet!' For those not fluent in Scots dialect, it translates as 'Dig away lads, I'm not dead yet!'

The disaster led to the 1867 City Improvement Act, which saw many of the semi-derelict hovels of the Old Town razed and replaced. On the reconstructed building at Paisley Close where McIvor was rescued, a stone was carved with 'Heave awa chaps, I'm no dead yet' to immortalise his call from beneath the carnage. The term 'lads' was apparently changed to 'chaps' to appease Victorian tourists. The building today is affectionately known as the 'Heave Awa Hoose'. Following the disaster, McIvor enlisted in the Royal Navy in 1862 as a Boy 2 class (cabin boy). But aged 23, in 1871 he deserted the Navy, and a £3 reward for his capture was posted by the *Police Gazette*. Avoiding the authorities, McIvor allegedly travelled to Liverpool and emigrated to the USA on the steamer *Samaria*. He arrived in Boston on 3 June 1871, where he apparently joined the US Navy.

Address Royal Mile, Paisley Close, 97–101 High Street, Edinburgh, EH1 1SP | Getting there Located above the entrance to Paisley Close; train to Waverley station | Hours Unrestricted | Tip Visit the Library of Mistakes, where tomes educate us how to avoid (repeated) economic collapse and financial catastrophes (33a Melville Street Lane, Edinburgh, EH3 7QB, www.libraryofmistakes.com).

68 Holodomor Memory

Millions of people killed by starvation

Ukraine is known as the 'breadbasket of Europe'. Yet, from 1932 to 1933, up to four million Ukrainians died of hunger due to a human-caused famine. The 'Holodomor' ('death by starvation' in Ukrainian) was part of a wider Soviet famine (1930–33) which affected grain-producing areas of the former Soviet Union (USSR). While Soviet policies caused the famine, it is still disputed whether the Holodomor was directly targeted at Ukrainians. Regardless, many countries today recognise the famine as genocide – that is, the deliberate destruction of a people.

Under Soviet dictator Joseph Stalin, Ukraine had been incorporated into the USSR in 1922. Stalin allowed some cultural autonomy in Ukraine, but by the end of the 1920s, Ukrainian identity was forcibly curtailed. At the same time, Stalin ordered collectivisation of agriculture, but rapid industrialisation of farming was disastrous. Ukraine was the biggest grain-producing region in the USSR and subject to unreasonably high grain quotas to the Soviet state. Famine occurred, and as Ukrainians starved their grain was sold abroad by Stalin. The starvation was selectively weaponised against Ukrainians for resisting Soviet policies and to supress nationalist sentiments.

Whilst the poorest in society were most affected, particularly in rural areas, even in cities corpses littered the streets. With reports of cannibalism and police ransacking homes of peasants and taking away anything edible, including pets, the famine peaked in the winter of 1932–33. The Holodomor provided a cover for a Soviet campaign of repression and persecution. Official silence and denial of the genocide by the Kremlin meant the Holodomor was not talked about until the Glasnost period of the 1980s. In 2017, the 'Eternal Memory' memorial in Edinburgh was unveiled. It is one of only two UK monuments to the deliberate campaign of starvation by the Soviet regime.

Address Holodomor 'Eternal Memory' Stone, Regent Gardens Entrance, 5 Royal Terrace, Edinburgh, EH7 5AB | Getting there Buses 1, 4, 5, 19 and 26 to Leopold Place; train to Edinburgh Waverley station | Hours Unrestricted | Tip Visit the grave of the 'Unknown Bairn', an unidentified boy aged about three years old found washed up on a beach in 1971 (Tayport Cemetery, Newport Road, Tayport, Fife, DD6 9AU).

69 James Lind's Memorial

The Hippocrates of naval medicine

Dr James Lind (1716–1794) is described as the Hippocrates and founding father of naval medicine. Born in Edinburgh into a family of merchants, Lind joined the Navy in 1739 as a surgeon's mate. By 1747 he became surgeon of HMS *Salisbury*, serving in the Channel Fleet. It was here that Lind conducted the first-ever controlled clinical trial of different treatments for scurvy.

Scurvy had plagued sailors for centuries. Thought to have been caused by an imbalance of bodily humours, scurvy is in fact a deficiency of vitamin C. This vitamin is found mainly in fruits and vegetables – food that was scarce on long sea voyages – and Lind discovered the linkage through systematic experimentation. He divided 12 scorbutic sailors into 6 groups. Each pair was given a mixture of acidic dietary items, such as vinegar or cider, or fruit including oranges and lemons. Team Fruit recovered from scurvy! Lind retired from the Navy, and in 1753 he published *A Treatise of the Scurvy*. His book offered remedies for treatment but was largely ignored by his contemporaries.

While not the first to find the link between citrus fruits and antiscorbutic effects, Lind offered evidence-based medicinal treatment. Scurvy caused pain, bruising, fatigue and bleeding gums among sailors. In 1740, during the War of Jenkins' Ear, Commodore George Anson's catastrophic circumnavigation saw only 188 sailors return out of a squadron of 1,854. Most had allegedly died from scurvy. Sailors at the time were 100 times more likely to die from disease than from war. With little concept of vitamins until Frederick Hopkins published his work in 1912, the Admiralty were slow in recommending citrus fruit as preventive medicine. A memorial plaque for Lind as the 'first experimental nutritionist' was unveiled at Edinburgh University in 1953. Sponsors of the plaque were the Sunkist Growers of Citrus Fruit of California and Arizona.

Address Edinburgh Medical School, Edinburgh University, Teviot Place, Edinburgh, EH8 9AG | Getting there The memorial tablet is in the main courtyard on the left side of the carriage entrance; national cycle route 75; buses 2, 9 and 47 to Bristo Square or 23, 27, 35, 45 and 47 to Lauriston Place | Hours Mon–Fri 9am–5pm, term-time only | Tip Visit the Hutton Memorial Gardens, a tribute to James Hutton (1726–1797), founder of modern geology and discoverer of 'deep time' (10 Viewcraig Gardens, Edinburgh, EH8 9UL).

70 John Knox's Grave

Buried in car parking space number 23

John Knox was a controversial leader of Scotland's Reformation during the 16th century. He led the Scottish process of breaking away from the Catholic Church. As founder of the Church of Scotland, Knox adopted a Presbyterian structure and brought in Calvinist doctrine, which emphasised the Bible's authority and sovereignty of God. Knox was influenced by early Church reformer George Wishart, who was burned at the stake by Cardinal Beaton in 1546 for heresy.

Little is known of Knox's life before 1540 or his family, though both his grandfathers fought and died at the Battle of Flodden in 1513 against King Henry VIII. By 1543, Knox was practising as an apostolic notary, suggesting he was in good standing with the ecclesiastical authorities. After Wishart was executed, a chain of events profoundly altered Knox's life. With Cardinal Beaton murdered by Protestant conspirators, Knox moved from place to place to escape persecution and arrest. Knox was eventually captured and sent to slavery in the French galleys, where his health was irreparably damaged.

After his release and periods of exile in England, Germany and Switzerland, Knox returned to Scotland and helped compile *The Scots Confession* and the ecclesiastical order of the new Reformed Church. He wrote his five-volume *History of the Reformation in Scotland* between 1559 and 1566. Knox served under Mary, Queen of Scots, though he admonished her for her Catholic support. He also called for Mary's execution after she was imprisoned for her alleged role in murdering her husband, Lord Darnley. Knox died on 24 November 1572 and was buried at St Giles. After years of development around St Giles, the original graveyard has been lost to real estate. Today, in a car park near St Giles, a marker in parking bay number 23 locates the approximate spot where Knox, the foremost leader of the Scottish Reformation, is buried.

Address Parliament Square, Edinburgh, EH1 1RQ | Getting there Buses 9, 23 and 27 to Victoria Street; train to Edinburgh Waverley station | Hours Unrestricted | Tip Visit the statue to James Braidwood, father of the British Fire Service, who set up the first-ever firefighting brigade in 1824 and who died fighting his own house fire (1–6 Parliament Square, Edinburgh, EH1 1RF).

71 John Livingston's Tomb

Black Death and an apothecary's grave

Nestled in a corner of Bruntsfield is a hidden garden dominated by a gravestone with a grinning skull and crossbones. This is the tomb of John Livingston (1592–1645) – an apothecary or chemist – who lived locally. Plague victims were brought to Bruntsfield, once beyond city limits, and quarantined from Edinburgh's residents. John Livingston treated those with bubonic plague.

Plague ravaged Edinburgh with frightening regularity between the 14th and 17th centuries. Known as the Black Death, the disease attacked the lymphatic system, causing swelling in victims' lymph nodes. Blood and pus seeped out of swellings, and fingers and toes turned black. Fever, vomiting, diarrhoea, and excruciating aches and pains followed. It often spread to the lungs via pneumonic plague, with death as the outcome. The first recorded plague outbreak in Edinburgh in 1349 saw two thirds of the populace die. In 1645, the final and worst outbreak occurred with around half of Edinburgh's 30,000 residents dying.

The 1645 outbreak was the first time city authorities gave dedicated medical support. Yet, the treatment was often worse than the disease, despite bubonic plague having a mortality rate of 50 per cent. Physicians relied on crude treatment methods, including painful bloodletting and boil-lancing with red-hot instruments. Corpses were buried in mass plague pits, near the present-day areas of Grange and Morningside. Treating plague victims in Bruntsfield, John Livingston contracted the Black Death and died aged 53. He was buried in a mausoleum built on his property. The tomb bears the Latin inscription: *Mors patet; Hora Latet* – 'Death is sure; the hour obscure'. It was not until the work of Louis Pasteur and Robert Koch in the 1800s that germs were found to cause plague. In 1894, the bacteria causing the disease was discovered by Alexandre Yersin, and named after him – *Yersinia pestis*.

Address John Livingston's Tomb, 1 Chamberlain Road, Edinburgh, EH10 4DL | **Getting there** Bus 5 to Greenhill Gardens | **Hours** Unrestricted, but best to visit during daylight hours | **Tip** See the Frederick Douglass Mural, a building-sized painting of the renowned 19th-century American abolitionist, known as 'Scotland's anti-slavery agent' (50 Lower Gilmore Place, Edinburgh, EH3 9NY).

72 Korean War Memorial

A 'forgotten' war that never ended

The Korean War (1950–53) was fought between (Soviet-backed) North Korea and (USA-backed) South Korea. Described by President Truman as a 'police action', as the USA never formally declared war, the conflict is known as the 'Forgotten War'. Compared with the global carnage of World War II (1939–1945) and the later angst of the Vietnam War, which succeeded it (1955–1975), the Korean War did not receive much public attention. A Japanese colony since 1910, Korea was divided into two occupation zones at the 38th parallel in 1945 by communist Soviet Union and capitalist USA.

During the late 1940s, insurgency along the border ensued. On 25 June 1950, under Soviet Union auspices, North Korea invaded the South to 'unite' Korea. With the USA intent upon containing communism, UN forces invaded. Apart from early advances by the North (supported by Chinese forces), combat became a protracted conflict along the border. With stalemate, an armistice was signed on 27 July 1953. However, a lack of a formal peace treaty means that the two countries are still technically at war. With war atrocities committed by both sides, North Korea was virtually destroyed as an industrial society. The USA dropped 635,000 tons of bombs (including over 32,500 tons of napalm), more than during the entire Pacific campaign in World War II.

On both sides, almost three million people died during the war, including 1,113 British soldiers, of whom 236 were Scots. In 2000, the Scottish Korean War Memorial was unveiled. Occupying a serene rural location on the edge of Edinburgh, a pagoda-style memorial echoes the Yin and Yang symbols of the Korean flag. Today, North Korea is a dystopian state, where citizens are denied basic civil, religious and political rights. The Demilitarized Zone (DMZ) border between the Koreas is still a geopolitical hotspot, where North Korea has now developed nuclear weapons.

Address Witchcraig Wood, Torphichen, West Lothian, EH48 4NP | **Getting there** Signed from Linlithgow town centre – from the M8 motorway, follow signs for Beecraigs Country Park | **Hours** Unrestricted | **Tip** Visit the Glasgow Korean War Monument commemorating dead service members where 'not one of them is forgotten before God' (Glasgow Necropolis, Glasgow, G4 0UZ).

73 Lt John Irving Grave

Serving on HMS Terror *led to terror*

For centuries, the fabled Northwest Passage (NWP) had frustrated many Arctic explorers. Through a series of sea lanes along the northern coast of North America between the Atlantic and Pacific oceans, the NWP offers a trade route to Asia. Christopher Columbus sought the NWP in 1492, while the first journey through the NWP was by Roald Amundsen during 1903–06.

In a quest to discover the NWP, the 1845 Franklin Expedition embarked with two ships – HMS *Erebus* and HMS *Terror*. Edinburgh-born Lieutenant John Irving (b. 1815) was appointed fourth in command of HMS *Terror*. Led by Sir John Franklin, the expedition set out with 128 intrepid souls. None would survive. The last sighting of the ships in July 1845 was off the coast of Greenland. After two years of silence, the Admiralty sent out a search party with HMS *Investigator*. After searching for the ill-fated crews, HMS *Investigator* became trapped in ice and was abandoned in 1853. Later expeditions revealed that HMS *Erebus* and *Terror* had been trapped by sea ice for 19 months and both ships were abandoned. A final note by Irving, known as the Victory Point Note, said that 24 crew were dead, and the plan was to trek to mainland Canada in a last-ditch attempt to survive. Autopsies of crew discovered through expeditions up until the 1980s found their canned rations had been tainted with lead, which caused botulism. Evidence of cut marks on skeletons and local Inuit reports suggest the last remaining crew resorted to cannibalism to feed themselves.

In 1879, an expedition by Fredrick Schwatka found a shallow grave on King William Island. It was thought to belong to Irving, though debates persist. Shown only by his medal, Irving's corpse was one of two from the Franklin expedition to be reinterred. Today, a tall Celtic cross marks Irving's final resting place at Dean Cemetery, while his comrades stay lost to the NWP.

Address Dean Cemetery, 63 Dean Path, Edinburgh, EH4 3AT, + 44 (0) 131 332 1496, www.deancemetery.org.uk | Getting there Buses 43, 47, 47B and X47 to Stewart's Melville; train to Haymarket station then a 20-minute walk; gravestone found near the west gate that leads to Modern Two Gallery | Hours Daily Oct–Mar 9am–dusk; Apr–Sep 9am–5pm | Tip Visit the grave of Robert Anstruther Goodsir at Dean Cemetery. He made Arctic voyages to look for his brother Harry Goodsir, who was lost with the Franklin Expedition and his body never found.

74 Mary King's Close

Tales of hauntings and Black Death

Hidden from view beneath the streets of Edinburgh is a cluster of underground passages. They are named after Mary King, an affluent merchant burgess and widow, who lived in the towering tenements from around 1635. Regarded as the world's first skyscrapers, over 600 inhabitants lived in the narrow streets in cramped conditions. The Close ran near to the old Nor Loch, a stagnant and highly polluted marsh. Noxious gas escaping from the Loch into the Close used to cause hallucinations. The streets became an open sewer as residents dumped their waste. Attracted by effluence, rats with fleas carrying the bacterium *Yersinia pestis* – causing bubonic plague or Black Death – meant disaster for the residents.

When the Black Death first appeared on the British Isles, it affected only England. Mockingly, Scots called it 'the foul death of the English'. The rats travelled north. In 1644, myth suggests that Mary King's Close was sealed off as the plague struck, entombing its residents. In fact, plague victims were treated with compassion and moved to Burgh Muir. Those left behind were visited by George Rae, the Plague Doctor. Dressed in leather and a bird-shaped mask, Rae administered his treatment by slicing off victims' sores and cauterising them with a red-hot poker.

In 1902, Andrew Chesney, the last resident, left and the Close was sealed. The Royal Exchange was built on top, and apart from being used as a bomb shelter during World War II, the close was not reopened until the 1990s. Today, it is a visitor attraction with re-enacted tales of the macabre. Visitors can 'ex-PEE-rience' the 'urine' of apothecarist Dr Arnott, meet 'Foul Clenger' Walter King, who cleansed homes of plague victims, or the ghost of 10-year-old Annie who succumbed to the Black Death. Visitors have reported a strange presence and cold temperatures, and often leave toys, dolls and sweets for her immortal soul.

Address The Real Mary King's Close, 2 Warriston's Close, High Street, Edinburgh, EH1 1PG, www.realmarykingsclose.com | Getting there Opposite St Giles Cathedral – car parking is very limited in the Old Town; train to Waverley Bridge station then a 10-minute walk | Hours See website for seasonal hours – pre-booking is recommended | Tip Visit the Blair Street Vaults, the largest system of ghostly underground caverns in Edinburgh (meeting point at the Mercat Cross, High Street, Edinburgh, EH1 1RF, +44 (0) 131 225 5445, www.mercattours.com).

75 Mini-Submarine Wrecks

Underwater warfare in midget submarines

Jutting out of the golden sands of Aberlady Bay, site of the first UK designated nature reserve in 1952, are two mounds of skeletal-like debris. However, this is not a cadaverous sea creature, but the wrecks of a World War II secret boat. The X-Craft midget submarines caused havoc to Nazi battleships, as well as attacking enemy-controlled harbours. Developed as fully functioning submarines, the X-Craft at 53 feet long and 6 feet in diameter could accommodate four submariners, including a commander, pilot, engineer and diver. In total, 23 submariners died during the war serving aboard X-Craft boats.

In September 1943, in the Norwegian Kaa Inlet, six X-Crafts attacked and scuttled the German battleship *Tirpitz* (sister ship of the famous *Bismark*) during Operation Source. The *Tirpitz* had been key in attacking allied merchant convoy ships – on which the UK depended for US and Canadian supplies – during the Battle of the Atlantic. Two of the X-Craft were lost with her crew. In 1944, the RAF further damaged the stricken *Tirpitz* during Operation Paravane and later sunk it during Operation Catechism. The attack saw Barnes Wallis' (of Dam Busters and 'bouncing bomb' fame) weapon used – the 'earthquake' bomb – codenamed 'Tallboy'. The daring X-Craft raid inspired the 1955 movie *Above Us the Waves*, starring John Mills. The X-Craft were also used as reconnaissance vessels for D-Day in 1944, taking samples of sand and soil from Normandy in condoms.

The X-Craft at Aberlady Bay are the XT type (T for training) and used to train crew as well as standing in for full-sized subs in naval exercises. Six XT-Craft were built by Vickers at Barrow. In 1946, two XTs were towed to the bay and used as target practice by the RAF. The wrecks stand as a tribute to those who sailed in such inhospitable vessels into the most hostile places.

Address Aberlady Bay, Longniddry, EH32 0QB | Getting there Car park off the A 198 (east of Aberlady); buses 124 and X24 to Aberlady Nature Reserve; beach is a 30-minute walk via a wooden footbridge, pass Marl Loch and keep left until the dunes; no dogs allowed on reserve | Hours Only visible at low tide, but be aware of tide times – check www.tideschart.com | Tip Visit the *Athena* Memorial Statue, honouring 81 women of Prestonpans executed for witchcraft during the 16th century (1 Dolphingstone Way, Prestonpans, EH32 9QX).

76 Monte Cassino Manuscript

Dismembered body and horrors of war

At St Mary's Cathedral in Edinburgh lie three impressive pieces of artwork entitled *The Manuscript of Monte Cassino*. Consisting of massively enlarged fragments of human anatomy – a hand, a foot and an ankle – the body-part sculptures are the work of Sir Eduardo Luigi Paolozzi. They stand for the horrors and futility of war that stem from Paolozzi's direct experiences of World War II and family loss.

Born in Leith to Italian immigrants in 1924, Paolozzi is widely seen as a pioneer of pop art. An art movement that appeared in the UK and USA in the 1950s, pop art challenged traditional fine art with imagery of popular culture. Pop art emphasised banal elements of mass culture through irony. Associated with mechanical means of reproduction, it was often removed from context or combined with unrelated items.

When Italy declared war on Britain in June 1940, like most Anglo-Italian men in Britain, Paolozzi was interned. During his three-month imprisonment, Paolizzi's father, grandfather and uncle were transported to Canada. They were among 800 others who drowned when their ship, the SS *Arandora Star*, was sunk by a German U-boat. While Paolozzi studied art during the war, in May 1944 the Allies launched the Battle of Monte Cassino – a town of Paolozzi's grandparents and a historic Benedictine monastery. Attempting to reach Rome, the Allies had to capture the 'Winter Lines', a fortification series on which Cassino lay. Towering at 1,706 feet, Monte Cassino and its hilltop abbey housed bones of the Benedictine order's founder, Saint Benedict. The ancient abbey was deliberately razed by Allied bombing. With 55,000 Allied casualties and 20,000 German casualties, the Battle of Monte Cassino is said to be the most gruelling, the most harrowing, and in one respect the most tragic, of any phase of the war in Italy. *The Manuscript of Monte Cassino* pop art borrows this pain.

Address Picardy Place, Edinburgh, EH1 3JD | Getting there Located in front of St Mary's R.C. Cathedral; train to Edinburgh Waverley station; tram stops are York Place or Picardy Place | Hours Unrestricted | Tip Visit the Playfair Monument commemorating John Playfair (1748–1819), a Scottish scientist and mathematician who was the first to propose that a river cuts its own valleys (Calton Hill, Edinburgh, EH1 3BJ).

77 National War Museum

Scotland's warfare and conflicts

Nestled within the walls of Edinburgh Castle, the National War Museum is dedicated to Scotland's many wars and conflicts over the past 400 years. It opened in 1933 in a converted storehouse built in 1748 for ordnance. The museum tells stories of war, combatants and the afflicted, through permanent and special exhibitions. Visitors are invited to explore 'state-sanctioned violence' of Scotland's involvement in war as a British nation. Military objects, artwork, personal stories and audio-visual experiences offer discovery of a nation in arms. Political and military relationships between Scotland and its powerful neighbour, England, are explored, along with the way in which the army represented opportunities for ordinary Scots.

Dedicated museums to warfare in the UK arose from the carnage of World War I. As the Western Front raged, the British War Cabinet decided to document the horrendous events. During 1917, efforts to record and commemorate sacrifices by all sections of society were made. This included exhibiting war from Scottish perspectives. Preliminary ideas for a Scottish war museum were started in 1917 by Alexander Ormiston Curle, a lawyer and archaeologist who rose to be Director of the National Museum of Scotland. His committee included John Stewart-Murray, eighth Duke of Atholl. However, in 1918, priority was given to constructing the Scottish National War Memorial to remember the war dead, which opened in 1927. The idea for a dedicated war museum faded.

So great was the slaughter of the war, the museum idea was resurrected in the late 1920s by the Duke of Atholl. Finally, on 23 May 1933, the museum was opened by Lord High Commissioner John Buchan as the Scottish Naval and Military Museum. Following World War II, in 1949, the Air Force was recognised, and the museum was renamed United Services Museum. In 2000, the museum changed its name to the National War Museum.

Address Edinburgh Castle, Edinburgh, EH1 2NG, +44 (0) 300 123 6789, www.nms.ac.uk/national-war-museum | Getting there Train to Edinburgh Waverley station | Hours Daily Oct–Mar 9.45am–4.45pm, Apr–Sep 9.45am–5.45pm | Tip Visit the Scottish National War Memorial, a commemorative symbol of the Scottish war dead (located within Edinburgh Castle, Edinburgh, EH1 2NG).

78 Old Calton Burial Ground

Monuments and graves of eminent Scots

The Old Calton Burial Ground on Calton Hill is the final resting place of many eminent Edinburgh citizens. In 1718, the Society of the Incorporated Trades of Calton bought a plot of land for use as a cemetery from the feudal superior, Lord Balmerino. They paid £1,013 (around £187,200 today). Expanded in the 1760s with screen walls added during 1816–19, burials ceased at the cemetery in the 1870s. The cemetery and its monuments are now protected as a Category A listed building.

Next to Governor's House in the south-east of the cemetery, the last remaining building of Calton Jail – once the largest prison in Scotland – stands the Political Martyrs Monument. Erected in 1844 and 89 feet tall, the obelisk remembers five political reformist men. Later known as the Chartist Martyrs, referring to the Chartism working-class movement aimed at British parliamentary reform, the men campaigned for universal suffrage. Brought before Lord Braxfield in 1793–94, the men were tried for 'unconscious sedition'. They were deported to Botany Bay penal colony in Australia for 14 years. Only one of the five men returned home.

The cemetery is also home to the only monument to the American Civil War (1861–1865) outside the United States. Dedicated in 1893, and with a figure of Abraham Lincoln, it remembers the Scots who fought and died in the conflict. A critical figure in the Scottish Enlightenment, David Hume (1711–1776), has his mausoleum in the form of a Roman tomb at Old Calton. After his death, his grave had to be guarded due to public hostility towards him for his professed atheism. Other notable graves include John Playfair (1748–1819), a prominent scientist; rival publishers William Blackwood (1776–1834) and Archibald Constable (1774–1827); and Dr Robert Candlish (1806–1873), a leading figure of the Great Disruption of 1843, an evangelical schism in the Church of Scotland.

Address Old Calton Cemetery, Waterloo Place, Edinburgh, EH1 3DE, +44 (0) 131 664 4314 | Getting there Buses 15, 26, 43, 44 and 113 to St Andrew's House; train to Edinburgh Waverley station then a 10-minute walk | Hours Daily 9am–5pm | Tip Discover how the first municipal fire service in the world started in Edinburgh by visiting the Museum of Scottish Fire Heritage (1a Dryden Terrace, Edinburgh, EH7 4NB, www.museumofscottishfireheritage.org).

79 Robert Burns Shelter

The 'darker' side of Rabbie Burns

Many memorials across Scotland commemorate the national bard, Robert (or Rabbie) Burns. Yet, in Prestonpans, a unique structure celebrates the beloved poet, and features artwork inspired by one of his best-known works. Erected in 1959, the Robert Burns Memorial Shelter consists of two windows and an entrance covered in metal bars. The main attraction, however, is held inside. In 2005, Kate Hunter created a mural depicting 'Tam O'Shanter', a long narrative poem by Burns. It narrates shenanigans of a drunk farmer and his friends in an Ayrshire public house. The mural depicts surreal imagery in which characters frolic with witches and bagpipe-playing devils.

Born in Alloway near Ayr in 1759, and dying at only 37 years old, Burns is regarded as a pioneer of the Romantic Movement. He had a major influence on poets Wordsworth, Coleridge and Shelley, among others. After his death, Burns became a Scottish cultural icon, as well as a source of identity for the Scottish diaspora. His sonnet 'Auld Lang Syne' (meaning 'times gone by') is often sung at Hogmanay events across the world. Together with an annual Burns Night celebration, Burns is often a product of 'tartanised tat' tourist souvenirs and exports of a kind of Scottish 'cultural imperialism'.

Regardless of Burns' revered status as poet and 'national rascal', his complicated character can be reviewed through a modern lens. With many illegitimate children, Burns committed adultery a number of times – even leaving one woman destitute. In an age of #MeToo, his sexual relations with his female servants might be seen as exerting power and misogynistic. Burns' mistaken views on slavery and empire have also been questioned, with charges of racism and illiberalism. Despite a 'presentism' perspective of morality and litigation, Burns was a flawed person. By present-day standards, he would certainly keep 21st-century lawyers busy.

Address 311 High Street, Prestonpans, EH32 9JF | Getting there Prohibited entry to shelter – mural can be viewed through windows and doorway and is illuminated at night | Hours Unrestricted | Tip Visit the Battle of Prestonpans Jacobite Museum, showing the first conflict of the 1745 Jacobite Uprising (Town Hall, 157b High Street, Prestonpans, EH32 9AY, www.battleofprestonpans1745.org).

80 Rosslyn Chapel

Suffragette bombs and alt-history

Built in 1456 by William St Clair (Sinclair), First Earl of Caithness, Rosslyn Chapel is a church of mystery and legends. The Episcopal chapel located in Roslin has become the subject of speculative theories and alternative history. Abandoned after the Scottish Reformation in 1560, Rosslyn was rededicated in 1862 after a visit by Queen Victoria. The chapel is still owned by the Sinclair family, who are descendants of Rognvald 'the Mighty', Jarl of Orkney – born in A.D. 835.

On 11 July 1914, a bomb planted by suffragettes exploded inside the chapel. From 1912 to 1914, as part of a campaign for women's suffrage, politically motivated bombings and arson attacks were directed at churches nationwide. It was believed that church authorities were complicit in reinforcing opposition to women's suffrage. There were 32 attacks on churches across Britain leading up to the Rosslyn bombing, including at Westminster Abbey and St Paul's Cathedral.

Rosslyn is full of architectural wonder and stonemasonry symbolism, and is a site of religious worship. However, it is alleged connections with the Knights Templar, the Holy Grail and Freemasonry that make Rosslyn a place of intrigue. Since the 1980s, these supposed connections were founded in comic stories of Batman, where the hero is caught up in a Scottish-clan vendetta, and an ancient treasure hidden in Rosslyn. But Rosslyn was made famous by the publication of Dan Brown's novel *The Da Vinci Code* (2003) and the movie that followed (2006). The story explores an alternative religious history where the Merovingian kings of France, protected by the Templars and Freemasons, were descended from the bloodline of Jesus Christ and Mary Magdalene. The novel takes in Rosslyn's hidden vaults as the place of the Holy Grail, the drinking vessel used by Jesus at the Last Supper, which Joseph of Arimathea used to catch Christ's blood at the Crucifixion.

Address Chapel Loan, Roslin, Midlothian, EH25 9PU, +44 (0) 131 440 2159, www.rosslynchapel.com | **Getting there** Bus 37 (towards Penicuik) from Edinburgh (Surgeons' Hall or South Bridge) or 140 from Musselburgh | **Hours** Mon–Sat 9am–5pm, Sun noon–5pm, booking recommended | **Tip** See Roslin's Gunpower Factory, opened in 1801 but now ruined, which produced explosives for the Napoleonic Wars up to World War II (Roslin Glen Country Park, Kirkettle Mill, Roslin, EH25 9QB).

81 The Soldier Bear Memorial

The bear that went to war

In 1942, the Anders' Army – a regiment of Polish POWs – travelled through Iran after being liberated from Soviet Gulags. On their journey, soldiers met a boy caring for a Syrian brown bear cub, after the mother bear had been hunted. Lieutenant Anatol Tarnowiecki bought the bear in exchange for a Swiss army knife and chocolate, and named him Wojtek (meaning 'Happy Warrior' in Polish). Wojtek became a mascot of the Polish II Corps, travelling to Syria, Palestine and Egypt.

Polish soldiers cared for the bear, feeding him condensed milk from old vodka bottles. As Wojtek grew up, he enjoyed drinking beer and eating cigarettes. As a morale booster for troops, Wojtek slept in the same barracks as the men and was taught to salute. When the regiment was called to fight in the Italian campaign with the British Eighth Army, British regulations stated no pets were allowed. To get around this rule, Wojtek was officially drafted into the Polish army with his own serial number and paybook. He was given the rank of Private and listed among the soldiers of the 22nd Artillery Supply Company. During the Battle of Monte Cassino, Wojtek helped his unit carry ammunition crates. In recognition of his service, Wojtek was promoted to Corporal, and he became the official emblem of the 22nd Company.

After the war, many Polish soldiers could not return home and settled in Scotland. Fearing that Wojtek would be used as Soviet communist propaganda if sent to Poland, Wojtek was given to Edinburgh Zoo. He lived the rest of his life at the zoo, often perking up at the sound of the Polish language, and died on 2 December 1963, aged 21. In 2015, a memorial to Wojtek was unveiled in Edinburgh, as a cultural symbol of unity between Poland and Scotland. The memorial is a touching tribute to the bond between animal and human, as well as cooperation between nations in times of crisis.

Address Wojtek Bear Memorial, 4 Princes Street, Edinburgh, EH1 2HG | Getting there Located in Princes Street Gardens; buses 10, 11, 15 and 16 to Princes Street West; train to Edinburgh Waverley station then a 10-minute walk | Hours Unrestricted | Tip Visit the Norwegian Memorial Stone, a tribute to Norwegian army units who trained in 'dark years of exile' in Scotland during World War II (located in Princes Street Gardens).

82 The 'Spitting Stone'

Spitting on the Heart of Midlothian

Edinburgh residents often spit at a heart-shaped mosaic of coloured granite. It can draw looks of bafflement from visitors to the city. The 'Heart of Midlothian' mosaic, set into the Royal Mile outside St Giles' Cathedral, marks the site of the infamous Tolbooth prison. For over 400 years, Tolbooth marked the administrative centre of the country and cast a shadow in the minds of locals who passed it.

Countless souls were incarcerated within its walls, many of them condemned to death at one of the city's execution sites. While the building was detested, the legend of the spitting tradition began after the Porteous Riots of 1736. During a public execution of three convicted smugglers, City Guards under the command of Captain John Porteous killed six people while trying to quell a crowd disturbance. The enraged mob started rioting and Porteous retreated to the City Guardhouse. He further instructed guards to shoot directly into the crowd, killing another six people. Porteous was later arrested and charged with murder and taken to the notorious Tolbooth. He was found guilty and sentenced to death but granted a reprieve by Queen Caroline.

Public resentment grew at the royal reprieve and on 7 September 1736, Porteus was hauled from Tolbooth by a 4,000-strong mob. He was dragged to the Grassmarket and lynched from a dyer's pole. Pulled down and stripped naked, he was hanged again. Porteus struggled free but was caught by the mob and beaten, breaking his arm and shoulder, and his feet were set alight. He was hanged again and died.

It was from this point, allegedly, that locals spat in disgust at the entrance of Tolbooth as they passed. In 1817, Tolbooth was demolished. In 1818, Sir Walter Scott's novel *The Heart of Midlothian* referenced the hated prison. It led to it being marked in the shape of a heart, where locals continue to spit their disgust.

Address Heart of Midlothian Mosaic, 197 High Street, Edinburgh, EH1 1RE | Getting there Adjacent to St Giles Cathedral; train to Edinburgh Waverley station | Hours Unrestricted | Tip See the 'Cutty Stool' in St Giles Cathedral, a piece of furniture that started a riot in 1637 that culminated in the 1639–40 Bishops' Wars between Scotland and England (St Giles Cathedral, High Street, Edinburgh, EH1 1RE).

83 Surgeons' Hall Museum

Death mask to human-skin book cover

From 1699, the Royal College of Surgeons of Edinburgh started to collect 'natural and artificial curiosities'. Originally developed as a teaching museum, the Surgeons' Hall Museum (SHM) opened in 1832. SHM houses one of the largest pathology collections in the world. The museum uncovers centuries of gruesome surgical development with a reconstructed anatomy theatre, as well as changes in dentistry. Exhibits include Joseph Lister and the breakthrough of antiseptic, and James Young Simpson and the discovery of chloroform. The museum aims to enlighten people of their health and wellbeing.

However, the SHM is home to a darker side of anatomy studies. The Robert Knox collection illustrates how Knox was a key SHM curator, but also his part in an infamous serial murder case of 1828. At the time, Knox was the most successful anatomist in the country, yet he was buying fresh corpses for anatomical dissection. Over 15 of these bodies were murder victims of 'resurrectionists' William Burke and William Hare. Knox was never charged for his involvement, but his reputation was severely damaged. He died in London in 1862. Burke was hanged and publicly dissected. His death mask and a pocketbook bound in his skin are included in the Knox collection. An inscription on the book reads 'Executed 28 Jan 1829', and there is a pencil inside. A children's song sings *'Up the close and down the stair / In the house with Burke and Hare / Burke's the butcher, Hare's the thief / Knox, the man who buys the beef.'*

Other grisly exhibits include the 'Sole Fish'. An angler in the early 1800s drew his net and grabbed a large sole. As the fish tried to escape, it jumped and forced itself into the fisherman's throat. After suffocating the angler, a post-mortem revealed the head of the sole near his stomach. Its teeth were fastened to the wall of the fisherman's gullet. The sole has been preserved.

Address Nicolson Street, Edinburgh, EH8 9DW, +44 (0) 131 527 1711, www.museum.rcsed.ac.uk | Getting there Buses 3, 5, 7, 8, 14, 29, 30, 31, 37 and 49; train to Edinburgh Waverley station | Hours Daily 10am–5pm | Tip See the skeleton of serial killer William Burke (Anatomical Museum, University of Edinburgh, Doorway 3, Medical School, Teviot Place, Edinburgh, EH8 9AG. Restricted opening times, www.ed.ac.uk/biomedical-sciences/anatomy/visit-anatomical-museum).

84__William Burke Museum

A 'bit of Burke' on gruesome display

Between 1827 and 1828, William Burke and William Hare terrorised the cobblestone streets of Edinburgh. Kidnapping and killing 17 people, they sold the corpses for anatomical experimentation and research. Peddling the dead to university anatomist Robert Knox for £10 per cadaver, Burke and Hare's bloodlust business was murder in the service of science. This was the age of 'resurrectionists' or criminal body snatchers, who stole the deceased from their graves.

Their heinous murders exposed shadows of the emerging medical establishment, during a period of enlightenment. Physicians such as Knox never questioned where the fresh corpses came from, as they tried to decode the human body through anatomical dissection. Yet, Knox was never convicted. Rather, he was protected by his lofty status and a seeming lack of evidence – though the case ruined his reputation and career.

Hare also avoided prison by giving testimony to convict Burke as the sole murderer. In front of thousands of spectators, Burke was hanged and dissected (like his victims) and his flayed skin sold or stolen as macabre mementos. Burke's skin was turned into keepsakes, including a pocketbook, which is shown at Edinburgh's Surgeons' Hall Museum.

Another item – a calling card – made from Burke's skin is found in the world's smallest museum. Within the esoteric shop of The Cadies & Witchery Tours, the only artefact on display is this ghoulish relic. Bought for £1,050 in 1988 from an auction house, the skin-made calling card was made from the back of Burke's hand. His skin was treated, tanned and decorated with gold tooling, which makes it even more grisly. The lurid calling card had been handed down the family of Piercy Hughes, a descendent of one of the surgeons involved in Burke's dissection. This 'bit of Burke' featured in the BBC's *Antiques Roadshow* in 2006, where it was described as 'priceless'.

Address The Cadies & Witchery Tours, 84 West Bow, Edinburgh, EH1 2HH, +44 (0) 131 225 6745, www.witcherytours.com | **Getting there** Bus 2 to Grassmarket or 23, 27 and X52 to Victoria Street; train to Edinburgh Waverley station then a 10-minute walk | **Hours** Mon & Tue noon–6pm, Wed–Sun noon–8pm | **Tip** Visit subterranean 'Goblin Hall', where necromancer Sir Hugo de Giffard practised his sorcery and allegedly raised an army of hobgoblins in 1267 (Yester Castle, Gifford, EH41 4PG).

85 The Witches' Well

Satanic panic of witchcraft

Nestled beneath the grandeur of Edinburgh Castle is the Witches' Well, the only memorial to accused witches in Edinburgh. The period between 1479 and 1722 is referred to as 'satanic panic', with most 'witches' persecuted in Scotland. Almost 4,000 people, 80 per cent of them women, were tried for witchery. Nearly two-thirds of the accused were executed, mostly by being burned alive. Almost a third of Scottish accused witches came from the Lothians. Witchcraft accusations were four times higher in Scotland then elsewhere in Britain.

Witchery was a belief that pacts with Satan and black magic acts were committed. The Scottish Witchcraft Act 1563 (repealed in 1736) was introduced during the reign of Mary, Queen of Scots. After Mary was executed for allegedly plotting against her cousin, Queen Elizabeth I, Mary's son King James IV enforced the witchery law with enthusiasm. Herbalists, vagrants, the mentally ill, political deviants or religious activists, or those who fell afoul of their neighbours, were often accused of witchcraft. To extract a confession, the accused were brutally tortured. Janet Horne from Dornoch was the last to be executed in Britain for witchcraft in 1727.

The Witches' Well, a cast iron water fountain (now dry), was commissioned by Sir Patrick Geddes in 1894 and designed by John Duncan to remember all executed 'witches'. Before the Royal Mile became a tourist hotspot, many of the witches were burned to death on the Esplanade below Edinburgh Castle. Without a funeral, their ashes were left to the elements. The unassuming memorial fountain is decorated with images of Celtic myths and legends, marking connotations of good and evil. A controversial plaque erected in 1912 above the well suggests some who were killed had magical powers and were guilty. Perhaps a more proper memorial to Scotland's tragic treatment of women is long overdue.

Address Castlehill, Edinburgh, EH1 2ND | Getting there Buses 9, 23 and 27 to Victoria Street then a 5-minute walk; train to Edinburgh Waverley station | Hours Unrestricted | Tip Visit the statue of David Hume, a philosopher of the Scottish Enlightenment, and rub his toe to bring good luck – a tradition that ironically defies Hume's rejection of superstition (12 St Giles Street, Edinburgh, EH1 1PT).

86 Woman and Child Memorial

Standing against racial discrimination

A statement of Scottish opposition to the (former) apartheid system of South Africa is made with *Woman and Child*. The bronze statue, sculpted by Scottish artist Anne Davidson (1937–2008) and unveiled in 1986, depicts an African woman wearing a headscarf, a plain knee-length dress and slip-on shoes. She is standing with her arm placed protectively around the shoulder of a young African girl. Behind them are two pieces of corrugated tin-roof panels, characteristic of South African townships and a symbol of poverty and racial discrimination.

Apartheid was a social policy implemented by racist South African politicians and made legal in 1948. Meaning 'apartness' in Afrikaans, a language derived from Dutch colonialists of South Africa, racial segregation of white and non-white people was institutionalised. An authoritarian political culture based on *baasskap* ('boss-ship') ensured white minority domination. Social stratification saw whites having the highest status, followed by Indians, 'Coloureds', then Black Africans. However, apartheid sparked significant international and domestic opposition, including condemnation by the United Nations. Nelson Mandela, a leading anti-apartheid activist was arrested in 1962 and spent 27 years incarcerated, mostly at Robben Island Prison.

Internal resistance during the 1970s and '80s saw brutal crack-downs and thousands of people killed. During the early 1990s, under President F. W. de Klerk, most of the social legislation that allowed for apartheid was repealed. In 1990, Mandela was released and became president of South Africa from 1994 until 1999, leading a policy of racial reconciliation. Today, South Africa still bears the scars of apartheid. Meanwhile, 'apartheid traits' have been used in other parts of the world, including the USA, Northern Ireland, India, and in the Israeli-occupied Palestinian territories.

Address Festival Square, Lothian Road, Edinburgh, EH3 9BZ | Getting there Buses 1, 10, 11, 12 and 15 to Usher Hall; train to Haymarket station | Hours Unrestricted | Tip See the *Branch Sculpture,* a figurative sculpture with echoes of Edvard Munch's *The Scream*, which mysteriously appeared without dedication in a cemetery (St John's Churchyard, 1a Lothian Road, Edinburgh, EH1 2AB).

87 WWI Training Trenches

Practising for the horrors of trench warfare

World War I was a war of trenches. Images of mud trenches along the Western Front are indelibly imprinted into our collective consciousness. Constructed with sandbags, wooden planks and tangled barbed wire, and just a few feet wide, trenches became trash dumps of the detritus of war. Broken ammunition boxes, empty cartridges, soiled bandages and human-bone fragments littered the trench system. Trenches were also dykes of despair, with men serving up to six days at a time, often under enemy bombardment. At 475 miles long, trench systems on the Western Front stretched from the English Channel to the Swiss Alps, although not in a continuous line.

While Western Front trench systems are well documented, less well known are the training trenches across the UK. These were extensive 'practice' trenches that were dug to train troops before they faced the real thing. With an influx of army recruits during the early stages of the war, the digging of practice trenches fostered team spirit as well as improving fitness. Trench warfare had long existed before the horrors of World War I. In A.D. 530, the Romans dug trenches at the Battle of Dara. In the Piedmontese Civil War (1639–1642), trenches as defensive measures were used. In the New Zealand Wars (1845–1872), the Māori developed elaborate trench systems, while massive trench works were utilised in both the Crimean War (1853–1856) and the American Civil War (1861–1865).

A surviving World War I training trench lies in the Dreghorn Woods, in one of Edinburgh's many open green spaces. The War Department had bought the Dreghorn estate in 1913. It was rediscovered by Lynne Gladstone-Miller, daughter of Captain Gladstone-Miller who trained in the Dreghorn trenches prior to being sent to France in 1915. The Dreghorn training trenches, despite being overgrown by nature, are now preserved to remind us of past terrors of trench warfare.

Address Dreghorn Woods, Redford Road, Edinburgh, EH13 0AT | **Getting there** Bus 16 to Redford House; noticeboards with maps throughout the woods – trenches are on the north side | **Hours** Unrestricted | **Tip** Visit the War Poets' Collection, a showcase of literary work of officers who suffered shell shock during World War I (Edinburgh Napier University, Craiglockhart Campus, 219 Colinton Road, Edinburgh, EH14 1DJ).

88 Cameronians Memorial

Respected regiment that refused to play football

The Cameronians were a British army rifle regiment. With roots back to the Cameronian Regiment (26th Foot) of 1689, they were the only British regiment with a religious foundation. Prior to forming the 26th Foot, soldiers were Covenanters who had rebelled against King Charles II for the right to follow their Presbyterian faith. As Protestant William of Orange ascended to the British crown in 1688, the Covenanters were incorporated into government forces.

Known also as the Scottish Rifles, the Cameronians were formally inaugurated in 1881 under the Childers Reforms. After action in the Boer Wars (1899–1902) in South Africa, Cameronians fought in World War I. During the famous 'Christmas Truce', a series of unofficial ceasefires along the Western Front in December 2014, the Cameronians refused to fraternise with the enemy. When Allied and German forces ventured into no-man's-land to play football, often seen as a symbolic moment of peace in the most violent of conflicts, the Cameronians refused to play. Growing up in the 'mean streets' of Lanarkshire, many Cameronians felt no inclination to be merry with men who had tried to kill them.

With 11 battalions in total, the Cameronians served in theatres of war including Gallipoli, Greece, Egypt and Palestine, while others served in India and Ireland. Over 7,000 Cameronians died and at least 10,000 were wounded during World War I. During World War II, Cameronians served in Madagascar, Persia (now Iran and Iraq), Italy and Germany. In 1924, a bronze memorial was unveiled to commemorate the regiment, with an inscription added in 1947. Rather than amalgamating with another regiment, they disbanded in 1968. The sculpture depicts a sergeant advancing 'over the top' (symbolising 'victory'), while a dead officer lies nearby (denoting 'sacrifice'). A Lewis gunner is shown offering covering gunfire for advancing troops.

Address 1425–1445 Argyle Street, Glasgow, G3 8AN | Getting there Memorial is located near Kelvingrove Art Gallery & Museum, Kelvingrove Park; buses from Glasgow centre include 2, 3, 4, 4A, 15, 77, 100, 189, X25, X25A, X76, X77 and M4; nearest subway station is Kelvinhall then a 9-minute walk | Hours Unrestricted | Tip Visit the statue of James Douglas, Earl of Angus, who was the first commander of the Cameronian Regiment in 1689 (Earl of Angus Monument, Blue Tower, Douglas, Lanark, ML11 0QL).

89_Cheapside Street Fire

Britain's worst peacetime fire-service disaster

Glasgow had a reputation for tragic fires up until the 1970s. Many fires resulted from poor building standards and premises being changed from their original purpose. Glasgow did not suffer from wartime bombing as other British cities did. Therefore, many industrial premises were of Victorian origin and found in narrow streets. The Cheapside Street fire on 28 March 1960 started in a whisky warehouse. More than 450 firefighters attended with every engine in the city. A million gallons of whisky in 21,000 wooden casks and 30,000 gallons of rum were housed in the building.

As the casks ruptured, they caused a massive boiling liquid expanding vapour explosion (BLEVE). The impact killed three firefighters instantly, while a further 11 died when buried in rubble along with three engines. The blaze spread to neighbouring buildings, including a tobacco warehouse and an ice-cream factory. It took a week to extinguish the fire. In total, 19 members of the fire brigade and salvage corps were killed. The appalling loss of life sent shock waves through the fire service. It confirmed many fears, including the lack of fire-safety legislation and fire inspections, and a need for a modern fire service.

A new programme for the fire brigade was launched later that year called 'A Service for the Sixties'. The victims were laid to rest at a tomb in Glasgow Necropolis. Firefighter James Dunlop, who survived the blaze, was awarded the George Medal for bravery. In 1968, in nearby James Watt Street, another tragic fire in a factory with barred windows claimed 22 lives. In 1972, the Kilbirnie Street warehouse fire killed seven Glasgow firefighters. The Cheapside fire victims were memorialised by a mosaic created by schoolchildren in 2010. The colourful mosaic features a saluting firefighter surrounded by flames and barrels of whisky. An official plaque is found close by.

Address Cheapside Street Fire Memorial Mosaic, Anderston Quay, Glasgow, G3 8BX | **Getting there** Located on the waterfront, close to the A804 bridge over the River Clyde; National Cycle Route 75 | **Hours** Unrestricted | **Tip** Visit the Glasgow Police Museum where the UK's oldest police force is revealed (1st Floor, 30 Bell Street, Glasgow, G1 1LG, www.policemuseum.org.uk).

90 The Coal Mining Monument

To all those who worked and died in mining

Profuse mineral wealth once lay beneath the county of Lanarkshire. Known as the 'Black Country' of Scotland, exploitation of coal saw a concentration of heavy industries in the area. But this mining of nature's treasure came at a cost, especially at mines around Cambuslang. Today, a striking memorial pays tributes to the men, women and children who worked and died in the coal mining industry. Dedicated in May 2005, the monument consists of a pit head winding wheel mounted on a base next to a mine cart.

Coal had been mined in Lanarkshire since the Middle Ages. In 1162, monks mined shallow-lying coal seams, while the first recorded mine dates from 1616. Collieries developed with the Industrial Revolution (1750s–1900), yet coal mining remained dangerous and harsh. With only candle or tallow light, miners worked in almost complete darkness. While most mining deaths involved men, many women and children were killed too. Before 1840, there was no inspector of mines, and fatalities were not officially recorded, though many incidents occurred. One of the first reports of a Scottish pit accident involved Janet Hodge on 10 March 1698. She was killed by a 'fall of coals', aged 47. On 4 June 1743, one of the first children to perish in a 'coal sink' was Andrew Morison, at Mellock mine.

Whole families often worked together at the colliery. Gendered division of labour saw men 'hewing' (cutting the coal) and women and children 'drawing' (moving the coal to the surface). Small children as young as five were used as 'trappers' (opening and closing ventilation doors). With stifling heat underground, women often wore little above the waist. Reported by a Government Commission, it provoked moral outrage in upper echelons of Victorian society. Yet for women it was a simple fact of survival in a world that lay beneath.

Address Cambuslang Miner Monument, Hamilton Road, Cambuslang, Lanarkshire, G72 7LD | Getting there Located behind bus stop near the Toll Pitch Pavilion; buses 7A, 64, 65, 164 and 165 to Christie Place; train to Cambuslang station then a 10-minute walk | Hours Unrestricted | Tip See an unusual statue of explorer Dr David Livingstone (1813–73) and two African natives being attacked by a lion (165 Station Road, Blantyre, G72 9BY, www.david-livingstone-birthplace.org).

91 Collins' Fountain

Ills of the 'demon drink'

Near to Glasgow Green – Britain's oldest public park and former execution site – is a monument to the ills of alcohol. The 1881 fountain memorial commemorates Sir William Collins (1817–1895), who helped build the Collins publishing conglomerate (now HarperCollins) and became Lord Provost of Glasgow (1877–1880). He was a staunch supporter of temperance – that is, abstaining from drinking alcohol. Collins was nicknamed 'Water Willie' for his avoidance of alcoholic drinks. Temperance fountains were installed to encourage people to drink clean water, rather than beer.

Temperance began in the 1800s as an American socio-religious movement to limit drinking. Scotland's first temperance society was founded by John Dunlop in Greenock in 1829. By 1854, the Glasgow Abstainers Group included about 40 societies who zealously 'took the pledge' to abstain from alcohol. Under the influence of evangelical religion with its sense of social outreach, temperance was a middle-class lobby against the working classes. Motivated by social order, and amplified by urban population growth, the bourgeoisie criticised widespread drunkenness among the lower classes. To social reformers, excessive consumption of alcohol led to poverty, neglect, immorality, disease and death.

Scots have long had a cultural relationship with alcohol. Between 1822 and 1829, at the beginning of the temperance movement, alcohol consumption trebled in Scotland. Deregulation of distillers and relaxed taxation provided cheap drink, though the temperance campaign ultimately failed in its aim of 'teetotalism' across society. Yet, concerns continue over the economic scale and health burdens in Scotland from alcohol-related harms. In 2018, Scotland was the first country in the world to set a minimum price for alcohol – a legacy, perhaps, of William Collins and his temperance goal of curtailing the 'demon drink'.

Address Collins' Temperance Fountain, Glasgow Green, Glasgow, G1 5LZ | Getting there National Cycle Route 75; train to Argyle Street station; nearest subway is St Enoch then a 15-minute walk | Hours Unrestricted | Tip Visit The Hunterian, the oldest museum in Scotland, with a 200-year-old collection of oddities and medical paraphernalia (Gilbert Scott Building, University of Glasgow, University Avenue, G12 8QQ, www.gla.ac.uk/hunterian).

92__Glasgow Necropolis

Sightsee in 'mansions of the dead'

In 1651, the rocky hill that overlooks Glasgow Cathedral was bought by the Merchants House (a group of wealthy city merchants). Planted with trees, it became known as Fir Park. In 1832, the Cemeteries Act allowed burial for profit and a competition to convert the park into a cemetery was advertised. Wanting to emulate the Père Lachaise Cemetery in Paris, John Strang wrote in his 1831 *Necropolis Glasguensis* that the cemetery would 'afford a much-wanted accommodation to the higher classes, be a lucrative source of profit, be respectful to the dead and be sanitary to the living'.

In April 1833, the Glasgow Necropolis opened for business as an interdenominational burial ground. Joseph Levi, a Jewish jeweller was the first burial and, a year later, Elizabeth Miles became the first Christian burial. Some 50,000 people have been buried at the 37-acre Necropolis. In the upper parts, imposing monuments of wealthy Victorians compete for attention. The tallest and most striking monument belongs to John Knox, a 16th-century religious fundamentalist and leading figure in the Presbyterian Reformation of the Church of Scotland. Other noteworthy structures include a mausoleum for Major Archibald Monteath (of the East India Company), and the 35-foot-high monument to William Gavin (a businessperson and religious controversialist). More modest memorials include William Miller, author of the nursery rhyme 'Wee Willie Winkie'.

During the early 1800s, the Necropolis saw body-snatchers, or 'resurrectionists', who stole freshly buried corpses to sell to university medical schools. However, the Anatomy Act 1832 offered legitimate opportunities, and the trade ceased. The 'Bridge of Sighs', named for being part of funeral processions and an allusion to its Venetian namesake, stands at the main entrance. Today, visitors cross the bridge and are invited to sightsee in the mansions of the dead.

Address Castle Street, Glasgow, G4 0UZ, www.glasgownecropolis.org | Getting there Main gates lie behind St Mungo's Museum of Religious Life & Art, next to Glasgow Cathedral; other gates via Wishart Street and John Knox Street; nearest subway station is Buchanan Street, then a 20-minute walk; regular buses, including City Sightseeing Tour Bus | Hours Daily 7am–dusk | Tip Visit the ruined 'Sherbert Factory', once the leading producer of sherbet in the world, which massively exploded in 1906 after Pineappleade was dropped in Powder Room B (6 Doune Quadrant, Glasgow, G20 6DL).

93 Glasgow University

Atonement for its slavery heritage

The evil of transatlantic slavery during the 16th to 19th centuries is woven into the urban fabric of Glasgow. Trade in tobacco, sugar and cotton made Glasgow wealthy. Buchanan Street, Glassford Street and Ingram Street are named after notorious exploiters of the slave market, while Jamaica, Tobago and Virginia are similarly commemorated. Slavery led to millions of people losing their lives, as well as decimation of cultures.

There has been a 'selective amnesia' about slavery heritage in Scotland. While Glasgow University was at the forefront of the abolitionist movement, the institution has a darker connection with slavery. In 2018, the university acknowledged it had benefitted financially from Scottish slave traders. Plantation owners and slave traders, such as Robert Cunninghame Graham, made a fortune from slavery. Selling his slaves in Jamaica, Graham returned to Scotland in 1772 and became Rector of Glasgow University in the 1780s. He sold his Jamaican servant for £100 and spent the proceeds on wine. Ironically, he made an endowment to the university for studies on political liberty. Graham was succeeded as Rector by moral philosopher and economist Dr Adam Smith, who became a leading voice against slavery.

In recognition of its 'difficult heritage', Glasgow University received up to £200 million from past slavery connections. As part of its 'reparative justice programme', the university has created an academic centre for the study of slavery, closer links with the University of the West Indies, and a memorial to those enslaved. A plaque is on display in the university Cloisters. While it was an economic phenomenon, slavery was not born of racism; rather racism was the result of slavery. The legacy of transatlantic slavery is institutional racism on an international scale, including pseudo-scientific racism that was used to justify the slave trade.

Address University of Glasgow, University Avenue, Glasgow, G12 8QQ, +44 (0) 141 330 2000, www.gla.ac.uk/explore/visit/attractions/tour | Getting there Buses 4, 4A, 6, 6A, 7, 7A, 8, 60, 60A, 61, 75, 90 and M3; nearest subway station is Hillhead | Hours Visit the website for details of guided tours – self-guided tours also possible | Tip See one of only four women in Glasgow to merit her own statue – Mary Barbour – a Red Clydeside Movement activist who helped organise the 1915 rent strikes (Greenhaugh Street, Govan, Glasgow, G51 3LA).

94 Ibrox Disaster Memorial

Sixty-six football fans who died in Stairway 13

On 2 January 1971 at Ibrox Stadium, during a Glasgow 'Old Firm' football match between Rangers and Celtic, 66 people were crushed to death in Stairway 13. It was known as the Second Ibrox Disaster; previously in 1902 during a game between Scotland and England, 25 people had died and over 500 were injured when a stand collapsed. Redeveloped in 1928, Ibrox saw the iconic red-brick grandstand constructed. With a capacity of 80,000 fans, the stadium was further enlarged during the 1930s. Few changes were made in the decades that followed, where fans were regularly packed tightly on terraces.

Yet, concerns of crowd safety at Ibrox were raised during the 1960s, particularly about lack of movement in the Stairway 13 exit. In 1961, two people were killed in the stairway. In 1967, eight fans were injured leaving the stadium. In 1969, 26 people were injured on Stairway 13 during egress. The 1971 disaster occurred as Celtic took a 1-nil lead in the 90th minute, and Rangers quickly equalised. Fans had already left, with thousands exiting via Stairway 13. A crush developed in the passageway, probably caused by someone tripping over, as fans piled into the exit. Most of the deaths were caused by compressive asphyxia, with bodies stacked up to six feet deep in the enclosed area. More than 200 fans were injured. All but one of the dead were male, with 18-year-old Margaret Ferguson being the only female victim. The loss included 31 teenagers, with the youngest to die being 9-year-old Nigel Pickup from Liverpool.

Rangers F.C. were found culpable for the tragedy and sued. It also led to government improvements in stadia safety. At Ibrox today, beneath a statue of John Greig, who was captain during the 1971 match, are the names of each victim. On every anniversary, Rangers F.C. hold a memorial service to remember the victims and the sad legacy the disaster left.

Address Ibrox Stadium, 150 Edminston Drive, Glasgow, G51 2XD, +44 (0) 141 580 8500, www.rangers.co.uk | Getting there The statue is found at the south-east corner of Ibrox stadium; buses 9A, 38, 38A, 90 and 121; nearest subway station is Ibrox | Hours Unrestricted but best to avoid home match days | Tip Visit Bill Struth's Grave, the final resting place of an unconventional Rangers manager who made his players wear a collar, tie and bowler hat for match days (Craigton Cemetery, 10 Cemetery Road, Glasgow, G52 1SJ).

95 Inveraray Jail

Penal codes from the past

On the shore of Loch Fyne in the heart of Inveraray is one of the best-preserved jails and courthouses in the world. Inveraray Jail has changed little since its construction, largely because the town of Inveraray has altered little. Inveraray Jail was commissioned to replace the old town house, which dated from 1755, and was considered too small for the prison populace. Original plans were for the jail to have three prisons; one for males, one for females and one for debtors (of either gender). But the scheme was too expensive and was curtailed.

Designed in 1820 by James Gillespie Graham in the Neo-Classical style, a second new prison building was needed in 1848. The Prisons (Scotland) Act 1839 meant that prisoners had to be separated from one another. With management of prisons from local authorities to the UK government, larger prisons were favoured. In 1889, Inveraray Jail closed, and its prisoners transferred to Barlinnie Prison in Glasgow. The courthouse continued for sheriff court appearances until 1965.

The idea of prisons as punishment was virtually unknown in medieval Scotland. In a feudal society where the king's barons had jurisdiction, once convicted, judgement was swift for offenders. They were either freed or hanged or dealt with in whatever manner seen fit. Pit-like castle dungeons held state and political prisoners, while transportation to the colonies was used for other criminals. In 1779, the Penitentiary Houses Act brought together Bridewells – places for vagrants and petty criminals – and early prisons. In the late 18th century, prison reformers like Samuel Romilly, John Howard and Elizabeth Fry campaigned for better prisoner welfare. Inveraray Jail was a result of this prison evolution. Since 1989, the jail has been a 'living museum' with visitors offered grisly re-enactments of criminal justice and incarceration during the 1800s.

Address Church Square, Inveraray, Argyll, PA32 8TX, +44 (0) 1499 302381, www.inverarayjail.co.uk | Getting there Disabled parking available and limited free parking | Hours Daily 10am–4pm; closed Christmas and New Year | Tip Visit The Drovers Inn, a 300-year-old inn rumoured to one of the most haunted hotels in Britain – just don't sleep in Room 6 (The Drovers Inn, North Loch, Lomond, Inverarnan, G83 7DX, www.droversinn.co.uk).

96 Jim Murray Memorial

A sport that can kill

Most professional boxers are lucky enough to make it out of the ring alive. Yet, it is estimated that over 2,000 boxers in the world died from the sport between 1720 and 2021. On Friday 13 October 1995, 25-year-old James 'Jim' Murray fought fellow Scot Drew Docherty for the British bantamweight title. At 5 feet 4 inches tall and with a total of 15 wins out of 17 fights, Murray was a rising boxing star.

Hosted at the Hospitality Hotel in Glasgow with an audience of 700, Murray was winning the bout on points. He only had to stay on his feet in the final round. However, after what looked like an innocuous punch from Docherty, Murray crashed to the floor. He tried in vain to rise, but the bell ended the fight. Medical staff rushed to a distressed Murray, hampered by a riot that had broken out in the crowd. He was taken to Glasgow's Southern General Hospital, where he had emergency brain surgery. Murray succumbed to his injuries and died two days later. Prior to Murray's death, fellow featherweight boxer Bradley Stone had died in a match in London in 1994. In response to both tragedies, Promoter Frank Warren set up the Murray Stone Foundation to finance MRI scans for every British fighter. Today, Murray is immortalised in his hometown by a life-sized bronze statue.

While the origin of boxing as a sport in unclear, early evidence suggests it began in ancient Ethiopia in the sixth millennium B.C. Spreading to Egypt, then to Greece and the ancient Olympics, boxing as a global combat sport has flourished. In 1887, the Marquess of Queensberry Rules were drafted to regulate boxing. Yet, despite improved safety measures, modern boxing is the only sport where professional athletes have reduced life expectancy. Sustaining head trauma in fights and training, a boxer's life expectancy is 67.7 years old, compared with a tennis player who can expect to live to 80.4 years.

Address Near Kildare Road, Newmains, Wishaw, ML2 9FB | Getting there The statue sits across from the A71 roundabout; buses 44, 266, 366, 367 and X11 to Bonkle Road; train to Motherwell station then a short bus or taxi ride | Hours Unrestricted | Tip See the 'Suffragette Umbrella Stand' at Glasgow Women's Library, a rich-in-meaning artefact saved from Duke Street Prison, which housed female political prisoners (Glasgow Women's Library, 23 Landressy Street, Glasgow, G40 1BP, www.womenslibrary.co.uk).

97 La Pasionaria

Fight against fascism

The statue of *La Pasionaria* (The Passionflower) overlooks the River Clyde. It depicts Dolores Ibárruri (1895–1989) in a striking pose. Dolores was a prominent Spanish anti-fascist propagandist during the Spanish Civil War (1936–1939). The war broke out after General Franco launched a military uprising against the democratically elected Republican government. It was a complex revolutionary struggle between classes, religions and political persuasions. The conflict was described by Claude Bowers, the US ambassador for Spain, as a 'dress rehearsal' for World War II. With a Nationalist victory and a brutal fascist dictatorship that would last until Franco's death in 1975, over 500,000 people died, with many atrocities committed in the post-war period.

While Britain kept an official policy of non-intervention, over 2,000 British volunteers went to Spain to fight against fascism. Many were killed in vain. As part of the International Brigades, over 500 Scots and 65 Glaswegians made the journey that had captured the imagination of the anglophone left. Ernest Hemingway and George Orwell famously joined the ranks to fight for the Republican cause. Meanwhile, Dolores Ibárruri gave inspirational speeches, including a farewell speech to leaving foreign fighters when fascist victory appeared inevitable. In 1977, having lived in Moscow, Dolores returned to Spain and was elected to parliament, aged 81. She famously said that it was 'better to die on your feet than live forever on your knees'.

Sculpted by Arthur Dooley, *La Pasionaria* was unveiled in 1980 after a contentious debate among local Glaswegian politicians. Many in the Labour movement supported the statue, while some Conservatives accused the council of erecting a 'horrid monument to a horrendous hag'. While the Conservatives vowed to fight for the statue's removal, *La Pasionaria* still stands proud today.

Address 286 Clyde Street, Glasgow, G5 9DA | Getting there Located on National Cycle Route 75 near Customs House Quay; train to Glasgow Central station | Hours Unrestricted | Tip Visit *Blockade Runners to Spain*, a memorial to British ship crews who defied Spanish Civil War port blockades to deliver supplies to Republicans (located at the junction of Broomielaw and Glasgow Bridge, Glasgow, G1 4QG).

98 Loch Long Torpedo Range

Military secrets and an executed spy

Opposite the village of Arrochar, the Loch Long Torpedo Range lies derelict on the western shore of Loch Long. The sea loch's name is not a reference to its length; rather, it comes from Gaelic for 'ship lake'. Prior to their defeat at the Battle of Largs in 1263, Viking invaders sailed up Loch Long before dragging their longships two miles overland into Loch Lomond. But it is the former torpedo testing range that holds today's military mystery.

Operating from 1912 to 1986, the abandoned range once housed Admiralty buildings and restricted areas. Weapon of choice for submarines that prowl ocean depths, torpedoes (minus their warheads) were test-fired down the loch. At its peak during World War II, up to 50 torpedoes a day were tested. The base was also involved in developing new weapons of war, including the first British electric torpedo. It also became a staging post for submarines on training manoeuvres, and the preparation of weapons for the Royal Navy. Development of superior weaponry and the need to test torpedoes at greater water depths meant that the range ceased testing in 1986. Some of its work was transferred to Faslane on nearby Gare Loch, home to Britain's fleet of Vanguard Trident submarines, armed with nuclear weapons.

During World War I, the range was at the centre of a remarkable story of a spy who achieved nothing yet paid with his life. German-born Uruguayan national Augusto Alfredo Roggen (1881–1915) travelled to Tarbet, close to the torpedo range. He had been under surveillance by British intelligent services, so was quickly arrested on suspicion of espionage. On him was a map of Loch Long, a revolver, invisible ink and a list of contacts. At his court martial, Roggen gave no statement or evidence in his defence and was found guilty. On 17 September 1915, he was sentenced to death by shooting by the Scots Guards at the Tower of London.

Address Off the A83, approximately 2 miles south of Arrochar, Argyll and Bute, G83 7AP | Getting there Nearest car park is Succoth Car Park, then a 15-minute walk; look out for unofficial pathways to the range – beware: the site is near deep water and has overgrown vegetation and neglected buildings | Hours Unrestricted but best avoided in the dark | Tip See 'The Tinkers' Heart', a rare memorial to the Scottish Traveller community, once a symbol of grief and loss but now a marker of love and peace (off the A815, near Cairndow, Argyll and Bute, PA26 8BQ).

99 Lord Roberts Monument

A statue to brutal suppression

Frederick Sleigh Roberts (1832–1914) was a Victorian-era military commander. Of small stature, Roberts was affectionally known as 'Bobs'. He was a revered military figure as the British Empire reached its zenith. Roberts led the East India Company (EIC) army, which was founded in 1600 and dissolved in 1874. The EIC functioned as a sovereign power on behalf of the British Crown and ruled the East Indies, the Indian subcontinent and other parts of Asia.

In India, fed by acrimony against invasive British reforms, harsh taxes and summary treatment of the aristocracy, many Indians revolted against colonialism. In 1857, the Indian Mutiny (also known as the Sepoy Mutiny), saw a major uprising that was brutally put down by Roberts and the EIC army. A grim feature of the rebellion was the ferocity that went with it. Mutineers killed their British officers and committed massacres against women and children. The British took vengeance by bayonetting hundreds of sepoys or firing them out of cannons.

With peace restored in 1859, the EIC was dissolved in India. Roberts went on to serve in Afghanistan, South Africa and Ireland. During the Boer Wars, together with Lord Kitchener, Roberts' strategy for victory included burning Boer farms and the internment of civilians in the first-ever concentration camps. Over 26,000 people, many of them children, perished in the camps.

Today, a 1916 statue of Roberts in Kelvingrove Park replicates a statue raised earlier in Calcutta in 1898. These monuments are of their time – fighting for an empire – where art and politics of the day intertwine within public space. The social practice of constructing such monuments stands for a dissonant heritage imbued with conflict. Today, however, it is questionable whether we should celebrate a person, who in the words of Dundee poet William McGonagall, 'spread death and desolation all along'.

Address Kelvingrove Park, Glasgow, G3 6DL | **Getting there** Buses from Glasgow centre include 2, 3, 4, 4A, 15, 77, 100, 189, X25, X25A, X76, X77 and M4; nearest subway station is Kelvinhall then a 9-minute walk | **Hours** Unrestricted | **Tip** Visit nearby 'Scott's Bench', a memorial bench dedicated to Scott Hutchison, lead singer of the band Frightened Rabbit, who suffered from mental-health issues and sadly died by suicide in 2018 – aged 36 (Kelvingrove Park, Glasgow, G3 6DL).

100 A Lost Roman Legion

The Ninth Legion that mysteriously disappeared

Most think that Hadrian's Wall marks the limit of the Roman Empire. Stretching across northern England, the 73-mile border built in A.D. 122 kept unruly Picts (an ancient Scottish tribe) at bay. Yet, Roman imperialists did venture into Caledonia (now Scotland). In A.D. 83 at the Battle of Mons Graupius (somewhere in the Grampians), the Romans slaughtered over 10,000 Caledonians. In the years that followed, the Caledonians regrouped and used guerrilla warfare against the Roman invaders. To protect Roman forces, Emperor Pius built the Antonine Wall in A.D. 142, a turf fortification stretching 39 miles between the Firth of Clyde and Firth of Forth. Abandoning it in A.D. 162, the Romans retreated south to Hadrian's Wall.

Further Roman incursions into Caledonia in A.D. 208 by Emperor Severus were met with fierce resistance. Afterwards, the Romans permanently retreated to Hadrian's Wall. Caledonia was never invaded again. With increasing attacks by the Picts (meaning 'people with painted faces') on the Romans, and with the 'falling of Rome', Roman rule in Britannia ended in A.D. 410. Yet, one of the enduring legends of Roman Caledonia is the disappearance of the Ninth Legion. Myth suggests that 5,000 men of the Legion were annihilated in Caledonia by Picts in the early second century. By A.D. 108, the legion was no more – presumably killed by barbarians of the Highlands.

Romanticised by Rosemary Sutcliff's novel *The Eagle of the Ninth* (1953) and the movie *The Eagle* (2011), the mysterious loss of an entire Roman legion in Caledonia plays to Scottish nationhood and identity. With Britannia succumbing to Roman rule, Scotland can declare to its historically troublesome neighbour, England, that it resisted one of the mightiest empires in history. Whatever the truth, the humorous sculptures by David Kemp in 1990, between Kilmacolm and Bridge of Weir, recreate the legion that simply disappeared.

Address The Lost IX Roman Legion, off A761, Kilmacolm, PA13 4RT | **Getting there** Sculptures found on National Cycle Route 75, approximately 2.5 miles east of Kilmacolm; accessible path; limited car parking at Knapps Loch, opposite B 788/A 761 junction | **Hours** Unrestricted | **Tip** Visit the Clochoderick Stone, where Dark Ages druids dispensed justice and the burial site of Strathclyde King Rhydderch Hael, who was active 532–614 (Crossflat Farm Road, Johnstone, Renfrewshire, PA10 2PF).

101 The Miners Memorial

To those killed in Scottish mining

Sculpted by John McKenna and unveiled in 2017, the Kingshill Miners Memorial is dedicated to those who earned a living underground and sometimes died in the process. Owned by the Coltness Iron Company, Kingshill Colliery 1 opened in 1919, while Collieries 2 and 3 opened in 1952. With a peak workforce of 1,496 personnel, as the mining industry declined, all the Kingshill mines were abandoned by 1975.

In 1959, 47 men died in Scotland's worst mining accident of the 20th century at Auchengeich. Following the Auchengeich Disaster, Kingshill Collieries were the first ever mines in Scotland to introduce 'self-rescuers'. These are portable pieces of equipment that supply breathable air when the surrounding environment lacks oxygen or is contaminated with toxic gases. After the Michael Colliery Disaster in 1967 in Fife, where nine men died from an underground fire, 'self-rescuers' were made mandatory at all Scottish mines. Other major Scottish mining tragedies include at Blantyre in 1877 (207 killed), Udston in 1887 (73 killed), Mauricewood in 1889 (63 killed), Stanrigg in 1919 (19 killed), Redding in 1923 (40 killed), and Knockshinnoch in 1950 (13 killed).

While mining has offered whole communities a sense of place and being, it is one of the most dangerous jobs in the world. In days when health and safety standards were not as rigorous as in the present day, Kingshill collieries saw its own tragedies. On 12 February 1924, Edward McFadyen (1884–1924) was killed in a machine accident while underground at Kingshill. Later in the same year, on 11 December, William Clemenson (1887–1924) was crushed to death by a roof fall. Similarly, on 23 May 1931, James Barr (1889–1931) died instantly when a coal seam collapsed. An underground fire on 13 November 1934 saw William Douglas (1904–1934), James McCallum (1912–1934) and Edward Stewart (1906–1934) killed at Kingshill.

Address Allanton Road, Newmains, Allanton, Wishaw, ML7 5AN | Getting there Buses 266, 365, 366 and 367 to Coltness Avenue; free roadside car parking | Hours Unrestricted | Tip Visit another John McKenna sculpture at the Auchengeich Miners Memorial, which commemorates 47 souls who perished during an underground pit fire (Gartferry Road, Moodiesburn, Glasgow, G69 0JG).

102 Overtoun Bridge

Dogs leap to a 'canine suicide'

Built in 1862 for industrialist James White, Overtoun House is a Scottish Baronial-style mansion. It was used as a convalescent home for injured soldiers during the world wars, and as a maternity hospital until 1970. Local lore tells of the spectre of the White Lady of Overtoun haunting the estate, the troubled grief-stricken widow of Baron John White who died in 1931.

However, an even-more macabre phenomenon has been reported at Overtoun. A bridge built in 1895 extends the driveway of Overtoun House, allowing easy access from the western approach. It spans a deep ravine and, despite the significant drop, foliage and vegetation either side of the bridge, gives the impression of level ground. Since the 1950s, anecdotal incidents of dogs mysteriously leaping from the bridge to their deaths have been reported. Tabloid newspapers suggest up to 600 dogs may have succumbed to such a 'canine suicide'.

Theories of why dogs seemingly feel compelled to jump over the bridge into the gorge include ghostly shenanigans. As animals are supposedly sensitive to the paranormal, it is said the White Lady lures the dogs to their death. Dog walkers have reported their dog 'freezing' on the bridge and staring at something hitherto unseen by the human eye. Some locals claim to feel dread while walking across the bridge. Others suggest residual odours of male mink urine agitates the dogs, sending them into a frenzy and into fateful leaps. Yet, the smell of mink at other Scottish bridges does not send dogs into hysteria. Of course, animals do not 'commit suicide' as people do. The truth might be that dogs confuse the lush foliage surrounding the bridge with ground level. Dogs see things from a lower perspective, which might create an optical illusion that the ground is close and flat. If they bolt over the bridge, dogs are unaware of the sheer drop. Dog owners beware!

Address Overtoun House and Bridge, Milton Brae, Dumbarton, G82 2SH | Getting there Car parking nearby at Langs Craigs Woods; bus to Milton then a 30-minute walk | Hours Unrestricted | Tip See the Memorial Cairn of John Cobb, accidentally killed on 29 September 1952 trying to beat the world speed record on Loch Ness (southbound side of A82, 1.5 miles south of Urquhart Castle, view from car layby opposite on northbound side of A82).

103 Paisley Witches

'Pain inflicted, suffering endured, injustice done'

At the junction of Maxwellton Street and George Street in Paisley lies an inconspicuous circle of cobblestones with a central horseshoe. This unassuming memorial marks the final resting place of seven souls who were executed as witches. The plaque reads: 'Pain inflicted, suffering endured, ínjustice done'. In what became the last ever mass execution of witches in western Europe, the episode began with a maid stealing some milk.

In August 1696, 11-year-old Christian Shaw, daughter of the Laird of Bargarran, caught servant Catherine Campbell drinking milk not belonging to her. After being 'grassed up' by Shaw, an angry Campbell wished for the Devil to 'haul [Shaw's] soul through Hell'. Shaw soon began to experience maladies of violent convulsions. Seeking help from Dr Brisbane, a renowned physician from Glasgow, Shaw engaged in desperate pleas with unseen tormentors. She was diagnosed as suffering from conversion disorder or Munchausen syndrome by modern medicine; yet she was believed to be a witchcraft victim. Accusations were directed towards Campbell, as well as Agnes Naismith, an elderly woman already associated with witchery. The witch hunt culminated in five others being accused – Margaret Lang, Margaret Fulton, John Reid, and brothers John and James Lindsay (aged 11 and 14 respectively).

Reid committed suicide, while the others were executed by garrote. John and James Lindsay held hands as they were hanged together. Naismith cast a dying curse upon all those present and their descendants. Numerous local tragedies, including the Paisley Canal Disaster in 1810, have been attributed to Naismith's curse. Corpses of the condemned were burned and ashes interred at Maxwellton Cross, the site of the Paisley Witches Memorial. Shaw, overcoming her 'bewitchment', became a successful textile entrepreneur and propelled Paisley to global prominence in weaving thread production.

Address Maxwellton Cross, 145 – 147 George Street, Paisley, PA1 2UB | Getting there Busy road junction, so memorial best viewed from pavement; buses 17A, 51A and 61 to Main Road or 17, 20, 20A, 61 and 340 to Newton Street; train to Paisley Canal station then a 15-minute walk | Hours Unrestricted | Tip See the Paisley Canal Disaster plaque, commemorating the worst tragedy of the canal age, in which 85 people died in 1810 when the *Countess of Eglinton* capsized in the Paisley Basin (1 Stow Brae, (car park) Paisley, PA1 2HF).

104 Pierre's Unmarked Grave

A poisoned lover and a Victorian scandal

In Ramshorn Graveyard lies a poisoned lover whose death featured in one of Glasgow's most sensational murder trials. Born in 1823 in Jersey, Pierre Emile L'Angelier was a lowly packing clerk in a Glasgow warehouse. In 1855, 32-year-old Pierre began a love affair with 19-year-old Madeleine Hamilton Smith, a Glasgow socialite. Her father was James Smith, a wealthy architect, and her uncle David Hamilton was a leading Neo-Classical architect.

As the couple came from different social classes, Madeleine had broken strict Victorian conventions. The pair would meet late at night, exchanging voluminous sexually charged correspondence. Madeleine would go on to lose her virginity to Pierre. Unaware of the secret liaison, Madeleine's parents arranged for her to marry socially acceptable William Harper Minnoch, to which Madeleine agreed. In 1857, she tried to end her relationship with Pierre and asked for her love letters to be returned. Instead, Pierre indignantly refused. He threatened to use them to expose her and force her to marry him. Madeleine was soon seen in a pharmacy buying arsenic. On 23 March 1857, Pierre was found dead of arsenic poisoning.

With the intimate letters discovered, Madeleine was arrested and put on trial. The letters caused a scandal. Although circumstantial evidence pointed towards her guilt, a verdict of 'Not Proven' was given. In the aftermath, Madeleine's family had to quit their Glasgow and country homes. Her father, broken by the affair, died in 1863, aged 55. In 1861, Madeleine married artist George Wardle. Under her new married name, Madeleine became involved with the Fabian Society. After the couple separated in 1889, she moved to New York and got married again, to William Sheehy. Madeleine died in 1928. Most modern scholars believe Madeleine committed the crime, but a lack of eyewitnesses and her high social class meant she got away with murder.

Address Ramshorn Graveyard, 98 Ingram Street, Glasgow, G1 1EX | **Getting there** Pierre's grave is close to the entrance in Plot J32 near the path with the name Fleming (who were family friends) etched; train to High Street station then a 5-minute walk; nearest subway station is Buchanan Street then a 12-minute walk | **Hours** Daily 8am–8pm | **Tip** Visit the former HQ of Professional Engineers of Scotland, now the Scottish Opera House, and see a memorial to the engineers who died on RMS *Titanic* (Scottish Opera, 39 Elmbank Crescent, Glasgow, G2 4PT).

105 Southern Necropolis

Home of the 'Gorbals Vampire'

The Southern Necropolis opened in 1840 and offered a decent place of burial for residents of The Gorbals. It replaced the Old Gorbals Burial Ground of 1715. Notorious for its poverty, The Gorbals on the River Clyde in Glasgow was once an affluent village. But, by the late 19th century, it had become densely populated as rural workers from the Highlands and Irish immigrants sought employment in Glasgow's shipyards and factories. Over 90,000 people lived in just 252 acres, compared with under 9,000 people today. As one of Europe's worst slums, up to 30 people used one toilet and there were 40 to a single tap. Appalling sanitation in the slums, and epidemics such as cholera and smallpox, meant that new burial grounds were needed.

If life was harsh in The Gorbals, then death was tamed by the new cemetery. With more burial grounds built in 1846 and 1850, and a grand gatehouse designed by Glasgow architect Charles Wilson, the cemetery has over 250,000 internments in its many lairs. The first burial on 21 July 1840 was that of the 16-month-old daughter of Archibald Cochran, who had died of croup. A notable resident is Sir Thomas Lipton (d. 1931), a yachtsman and philanthropist, and founder of the Lipton Tea Company. He was the most persistent challenger in the history of the America's Cup yacht race, having lost five straight races.

In 1954, the Southern Necropolis hosted young 'vampire' hunters. Rumours had spread among children that a terrible seven-foot vampire with iron teeth was roaming the graveyard. Tales of the vampire murdering two boys and feasting on their corpses abounded. Intent on bringing the 'Gorbals Vampire' to justice, children armed with blades, stakes and crosses descended on the cemetery. As youngsters hunted the vampire, hysteria spread throughout The Gorbals. The episode fostered a debate about the impacts of American horror comics on young people.

Address 3 Southern Necropolis Gate Lodge, Caledonia Road, Glasgow, G5 0JQ, +44 (0) 141 287 3961, www.southernnecropolis.co.uk | **Getting there** Bus 267; train to Glasgow Central station then a 30-minute walk | **Hours** Daily 7am–4.30pm; visit website for bespoke tours | **Tip** Visit the 'White Lady' monument at Southern Necropolis, grave of Mary McNaughton who was killed in a tramcar accident in 1933. Walk round her three times, or she is said to turn your body to stone!

106 St Valentine's Bones

Trading body parts as holy relics

Behind the romantic façade of Valentine's Day, the world's largest festival of love held annually on 14 February, is a grisly tale. Alongside boxes of chocolates, candlelit meals and notes of affection is a story of body parts scattered across Europe, and a beheading. According to legend, the Catholic martyr Saint Valentine was executed on 14 February A.D. 270 for refusing to renounce his faith. He supposedly broke a Roman ban on performing marriages for persecuted Christians. In A.D. 496, Pope Gelasius made Valentine's execution date a Catholic feast day in honour of his martyrdom. Valentine became the patron saint of lovers – as well as epileptics and beekeepers.

In the 14th century, Valentine's Day was championed by 'father of English literature' Geoffrey Chaucer (1343–1400). Best known for writing *The Canterbury Tales*, the English author wrote *Parlement of Foules* (modernised as *Parliament of Fowls*), which had the first-ever mention that St Valentine's Day was special for lovers. Later in the Victorian era, exchanging lace-adorned cards between the genders became common. Today, commercialisation of St Valentine's has made love and affection tangible with mass-produced trinkets.

Yet, it was Valentine's bones that offered the earliest trade as holy relics. Pilgrims have long flocked to see his skull at the Basilica di San Valentino in Terni (Italy), his heart at a Dublin shrine, his shoulder bone in a Prague chapel, and his other remains in a Madrid church. In 1868, the Franciscans brought Valetine's forearm to St Francis' Church in Glasgow. In 1993, the relic was moved to the Blessed John Duns Scotus Church in The Gorbals. Given the uncertainty of where Valentine's remains are, or who he was, many churches claim his relics as an attraction. With a trade in (holy) bodies, the church has made money through increased pilgrimages – akin to modern tourism today!

Address The Franciscan Friary, 270 Ballater Street, The Gorbals, Glasgow, G5 0YT, +44 (0) 141 429 0740 | Getting there Buses 65 and 164 to Florence Street; train to Bridgeton station then a 25-minute walk | Hours Mon–Fri 8.30am–5pm | Tip Visit the grave of John Brown (d. 1835), who was trapped for 23 days underground after a mine collapse and died 3 days after rescue (Dailly Cemetery, Girvan, KA26 9SB).

107 Stillborn Baby Memorial

For our babies briefly known but never forgotten

Sadly, the death of a baby is not a rare event. Every day in the UK, around 13 babies die shortly before, during or soon after birth. According to the Stillborn and Neonatal Death Society (SANDS), 2,866 stillbirths were recorded in the UK in 2021. Cause of death for one-third of stillbirths is unknown, with another third being caused by placenta problems. There is still much uncertainty over the numbers and rates of pregnancy loss, with evidence suggesting 15 out of every 100 pregnancies end in miscarriage in the UK. Since 1992 in the UK, if a baby is born dead before 24 completed weeks of pregnancy (legally described as a 'late miscarriage'), then the death cannot be registered, but a funeral can take place. If a baby is stillborn after 24 weeks, or was born alive then died, the death must be registered, and the baby must be formally buried or cremated by law.

Until the mid-1980s, stillbirths were not seen as a major bereavement. Babies born dead at any gestation were swiftly removed from labour wards, with little or no opportunity for parents to see their baby. Communal unmarked graves, with limited records, were used for death disposal. Sometimes stillborn babies were placed in a coffin of unrelated women who had recently died. Families of the stillborn were left isolated, and it is difficult to find pre-1992 stillborn final resting places.

Despite clinical methods of the past, bereaved parents today are encouraged to see and hold their baby, to offer a name, to collect keepsakes in 'memory boxes', and make personal decisions about funerals and memorials. In 1998, a campaign for a Stillborn Memorial by Glasgow Councillor Elaine Smith, the Drumchapel Child Bereavement Support Group and SANDS was launched. Unveiled in 1999, this poignant memorial sits at the entrance of Glasgow Necropolis commemorating over 250 stillbirths across the city.

Address The Glasgow Necropolis, Castle Street, Glasgow, G4 0UZ, www.glasgownecropolis.org | **Getting there** The Stillborn Baby Memorial is found at the Church Lane entrance of the Necropolis | **Hours** Daily 7am–dusk | **Tip** If you have been affected by past or recent stillbirth in the UK, please visit Brief Lives Remembered (www.brieflives-remembered.co.uk), or SANDS (www.sands.org.uk) or call/email the SANDS Helpline +44 (0) 808 164 3332/helpline@sands.org.uk.

108 Victoria Cross Memorial

Awarded for 'valour in the presence of the enemy'

The Victoria Cross (VC) is the most prestigious award of the British decorations systems. Awarded to British Armed Forces of any rank or any civilian under military command, the medal can be bestowed posthumously. Before the Crimean War (1853–56), other European countries had awards that did not discriminate against class or rank, including the French 'Legion of Honour' (established 1802) and the Dutch 'Order of William' (established 1815). The VC was introduced in 1856 by Queen Victoria to honour acts of valour during the Crimean War. No civilian has received the award since 1879, while the medal has been awarded 1,358 times to 1,355 individuals. Only 15 awards have been made since World War II.

Captain Harry Ranken of the Royal Medical Corps was the first Glaswegian to receive the VC. In September 1914 at Haute-Avesnes, France, Captain Ranken was wounded while attending to his patients on the battlefield. Under heavy fire, he sacrificed his own chance of survival to attend to their needs. When he was finally carried off, his wounds were too severe, and he later died.

In 2007, a VC Memorial was unveiled at the Necropolis to commemorate 29 VC holders from the Glasgow area. It was erected by the city council at the suggestion of Tom Healy, a VC enthusiast, after he discovered one of the first VC recipients was from Glasgow. James McKechnie VC of the Scots Guards was buried in an unmarked pauper's grave within the Necropolis. Carved in polished grey granite, the memorial is an enlarged version of the medal, with its famous lion, crown and inscription: *For Valour*. However, the design of the VC was originally greeted with little enthusiasm by the *Glasgow Herald* on 1 July 1857. The newspaper said the VC medal was a 'dull, heavy and tasteless affair… for the VC is the shabbiest of all prizes'. Today, the VC is highly prized, with some valued at millions of pounds.

Address The Glasgow Necropolis, Church Lane, Glasgow, G4 0UZ, www.glasgownecropolis.org | **Getting there** The memorial is found at the north side of the approach road from the Cathedral; regular bus services, including City Sightseeing Tour Bus; nearest subway station is Buchanan Street, then a 20-minute walk | **Hours** Daily 7am–dusk | **Tip** Visit Mugdock Gunsite and the remains of a World War II anti-aircraft battery to protect Glasgow and the Clyde Basin (Mugdock Country Park, Milngavie, Mugdock, Glasgow, G62 8EL, www.mugdock-country-park.org.uk).

109 Wallace's Well

Wallace's final drink as a free man

William Wallace is often portrayed as a roving vagabond who fought against English rule in the late 13th century. Yet, Sir William Wallace (born c. 1270, probably near Paisley) came from the lesser aristocracy. Wallace was the second son of Sir Malcolm Wallace of Elderslie. Sir Malcom was a minor landowner and a vassal (feudal land owner) to James, the fifth steward of Scotland. But, when King Edward I deposed the Scottish king John de Balliol in 1296, after he made an 'Auld Alliance' with Edward's enemy the King of France, William Wallace entered battle as resistance leader and became a national hero.

However, Sir William Wallace as a Scottish knight was not invincible, despite the mystery that surrounds him. With a famous victory against the English at the Battle of Stirling Bridge in 1297, Wallace was later defeated at the Battle of Falkirk in 1298. Fleeing to France in 1299 and possibly to Rome, Wallace returned to Scotland in 1303. By this time, most Scottish lords had pledged allegiance to Edward I. Wallace also had a huge bounty on his head – to be killed or captured.

In 1305, while staying at a farm in 'Rab Rae's Toun', now Robroyston in Glasgow, Wallace was betrayed. He is said to have drunk from a nearby well, his final drink as a free man. Seized in his bed, and with his friend Kerlie killed near the well, Wallace was betrayed by servant Jack Short or farm owner Rab Rae. He was handed to Scottish nobleman Sir John Menteith, then to the English. He was executed at The Elms in London, where Smithfield Market now stands. Immortalised in a 1477 poem 'The Wallace' by Scots bard Blind Harry, 'Wallace's Well' is a marker in Scottish national memory. Delisted as a protected site in 1993, the well has seen local activism to save it from development. Today, tourism keeps alive memory of the well and of Wallace, a martyr to Scottish nationhood.

Address Langmuirhead Road, Robroyston, Glasgow, G33 1FA, www.clanwallace.org | Getting there Buses 19 and 19A to Robroyston; train to Robroyston from Glasgow Queen Street station | Hours Unrestricted | Tip Visit nearby Wallace Monument marking the farm where Sir William Wallace was captured (Lumloch Road, Robroyston, Glasgow, G64 1UW, www.robroyston.org).

110 The Witch's Skull

A female skull in Glasgow's only pub museum

Known locally as the 'Sarry Heid' or 'Sorry Head', The Saracen Head public house was established in 1755. This former coaching inn – described by some as 'rough' – is more than a modern drinking den. Frequented by football fans on Celtic match days, the pub is Glasgow's first (and perhaps only) 'pub museum'. A poem by national bard Robert Burns, once shown at the pub, is said to be in the owner's hands for safekeeping. But, within a display case near the bar, perched upon a metal tankard is a blackened human skull.

Attributed to Maggie Wall, a woman accused of witchcraft and burned alive in 1657, the skull takes pride of place in this characterful pub. A mysterious monument to Maggie Wall, with no records of her existence, is at Dunning in Perthshire. However, Glaswegian urban myth has the skull at The Saracen Head as belonging to Maggie. While the skull is real, Maggie's skull is unlikely to have survived any conflagration. Instead, it is likely that the skull was taken as a macabre keepsake from nearby Church of Little St Mungo. Whatever the case, the skull acts as a symbolic *memento mori* ('remember that you will die'). It also serves to remind us of the many people (mostly women) accused of witchery between the 1500s and 1700s, and who were executed.

During the Abbasid Caliphates from the 8th to 17th centuries, *Saracen* described anyone who followed Islam, where Saracen was derived from *Sarakene* in northern Saudi Arabia. Legend has it that anyone returning from the Crusades of the Middle Ages with a 'Saracen's head' was considered a conquering hero. Enshrined through inn names, The Saracen Head in Glasgow has welcomed guests such as Samuel Johnson, the purveyor of the English dictionary, Adam Smith, the father of economics, and poet William Wordsworth. More recent celebrities to visit the pub have included the Big Yin, otherwise known as comedian Sir Billy Connolly.

Address The Saracen Head, 209 Gallowgate, Calton, Glasgow, G1 5DX, +44 (0) 141 552 1660, www.saracenhead.com | Getting there Buses 18, 26, 61 and 240; train to High Street (Glasgow) station; best to avoid Celtic FC home days | Hours Mon 11am–9pm, Tue–Sat 11am–11pm, Sun noon–10.30pm | Tip Visit the Sharmanka Kinetic Theatre, where elaborate clockwork contraptions create small worlds of horror and ghoulish inventions (Sharmanka Kinetic Theatre, 103 Trongate, Glasgow, G1 5HD, www.sharmanka.com).

111 Women of the Necropolis

From a witch to medical pioneer to gypsy queen

In a patriarchal world where males often dominate the living as well as the dead, the female voice is often unheard. In Glasgow's Necropolis, some 50,000 souls are buried with 3,500 monuments commemorating the great and the good, mostly men. Before the Necropolis opened in 1833, urban cemetery tales were of shallow graves and protruding bones and noxious fumes. Yet, with death made both hygienic and picturesque in the new cemetery, headstones of most women are acknowledged only by their roles as wives and daughters.

However, wandering the 'city of the dead', notable exceptions are visible. Just outside the cemetery, near Glasgow Cathedral, is a monument to the medieval Bishop's Palace. Here, women accused of witchcraft were imprisoned. In 1597, Margaret Aitken, 'The Great Witch of Balwearie' of Fife, claimed she could recognise other witches by marks in their eyes. When Aitken visited Glasgow, Minister John Cowper condemned many innocent women to death on her 'evidence'. The resultant outcry prompted an inquiry into the reliability of witches' testimonies.

Inside the cemetery is a memorial to Corlinda Lee (1831–1900), 'Queen of the Gypsies'. When Lee married horse trainer George Smith, she merged two important gypsy dynasties. Capitalising on Victorian fascination with gypsy life, Lee even read Queen Victoria's palm. Marion Gilchrist (1864–1952) is also buried at the Necropolis. She was the first female graduate of the University of Glasgow, and one of the first to qualify in medicine from a Scottish university. Gilchrist went on to become a leading activist in the Women's Suffrage Movement. Meanwhile, close to the imposing John Knox monument is a simple gravestone having no dedication beyond an image of four children and the words 'beloved mother'. Research has shown the grave belongs to Agnes Strang, a woman who died in childbirth in the winter of 1849.

Address The Glasgow Necropolis, Castle Street, Glasgow, G4 0UZ, www.glasgownecropolis.org | Getting there Main gates lie behind St Mungo's Museum of Religious Life and Art, next to Glasgow Cathedral; other gates via Wishart Street & John Knox Street; regular bus services, including City Sightseeing Tour Bus; nearest subway station is Buchanan Street, then a 20-minute walk | Hours Daily 7am–dusk | Tip Visit University of Glasgow's 'Memorial Gates' inscribed with names of 29 outstanding figures from the university's first 500 years, including Isabella Elder, a suffragette, shipyard owner and benefactor of women's education (University of Glasgow, 82 Hillhead Street, Glasgow, G12 8QQ).

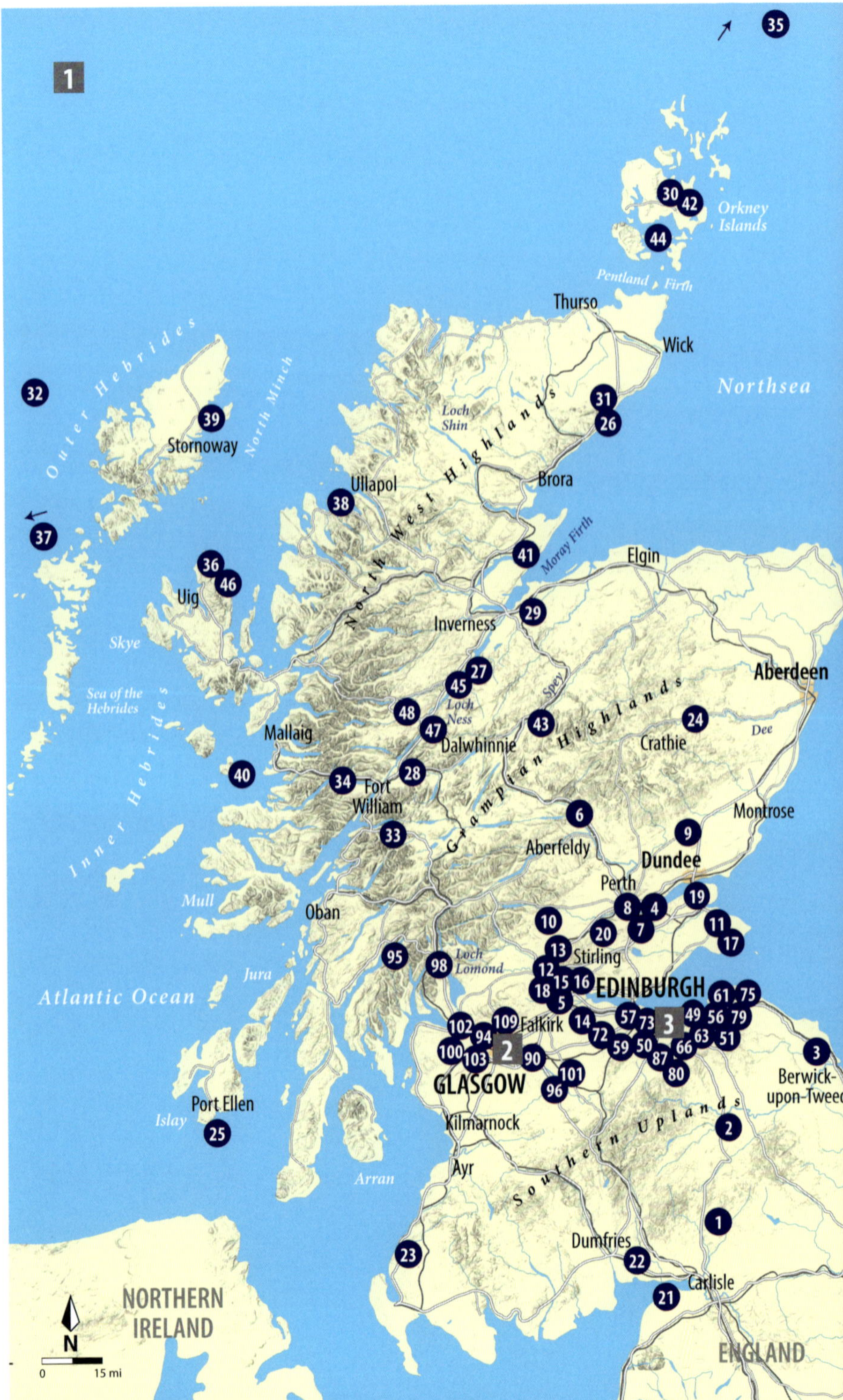

1
35
30
42
Orkney Islands
44
Pentland Firth
Thurso
Wick
Northsea
Outer Hebrides
North Minch
32
39
Stornoway
Loch Shin
31
26
North West Highlands
Ullapol
38
Brora
37
Moray Firth
41
Elgin
36
46
Uig
29
Inverness
Skye
27
45
Loch Ness
Aberdeen
Sea of the Hebrides
Spey
48
47
43
24
Mallaig
Dalwhinnie
Grampian Highlands
Crathie
Dee
Inner Hebrides
40
34
Fort William
28
6
Montrose
33
9
Aberfeldy
Dundee
Perth
19
Mull
Oban
8
4
10
7
11
20
17
13
Stirling
95
98
Loch Lomond
Jura
12
15
16
18
EDINBURGH
61
75
Atlantic Ocean
5
102
109
Falkirk
14
57
73
3
49
56
79
94
72
63
51
100
2
59
50
66
103
90
87
3
80
101
GLASGOW
96
Berwick-upon-Tweed
Port Ellen
Islay
25
Kilmarnock
Southern Uplands
2
Ayr
Arran
1
Dumfries
23
22
Carlisle
21
NORTHERN IRELAND
N
0
15 mi
ENGLAND

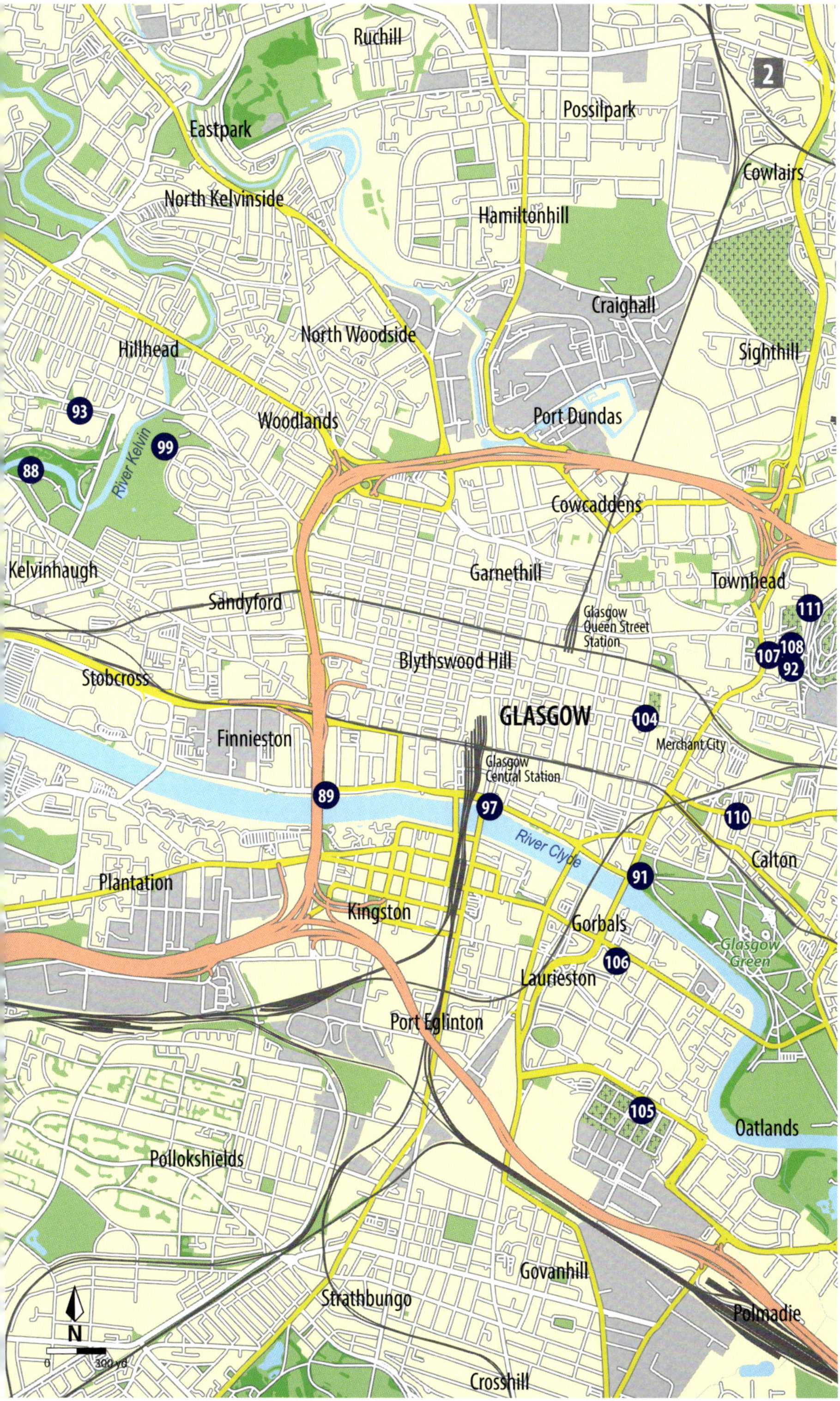
2
Ruchill
Possilpark
Eastpark
Cowlairs
North Kelvinside
Hamiltonhill
Craighall
Sighthill
North Woodside
Hillhead
Port Dundas
Woodlands
93
99
88
River Kelvin
Cowcaddens
Kelvinhaugh
Garnethill
Townhead
Sandyford
Glasgow Queen Street Station
111
108
107
92
Blythswood Hill
Stobcross
GLASGOW
104
Merchant City
Finnieston
Glasgow Central Station
89
97
110
River Clyde
Calton
91
Plantation
Kingston
Gorbals
Glasgow Green
106
Laurieston
Port Eglinton
105
Oatlands
Pollokshields
Govanhill
Strathbungo
Polmadie
N
0
300 yd
Crosshill

3
Royal Botanic Garden
Inverleith Row
Broughton Road
Leith Walk
Henderson Row
Broughton Street
New Town
68
76
Calton Hill
Queen Street Gardens
Hanover Street
Queen Street
Regent Road
78
EDINBURGH
Queensferry Street
Princes Street
Princes Street Gardens
81
67
Holyrood Road
74
82
70
77
54
85
Lawnmarket
84
Old Town
58
60
64
53
62
86
Lothian Road
65
Nicolson Street
Pleasance
Salisbury Crags
83
55
52
Lauriston Place
69
The Meadows
Melville Drive
Grange Road
Minto Street
71
N
0
200 yd

Philip R. Stone
111 Dark Places in England That You Shouldn't Miss
ISBN 978-3-7408-0900-3

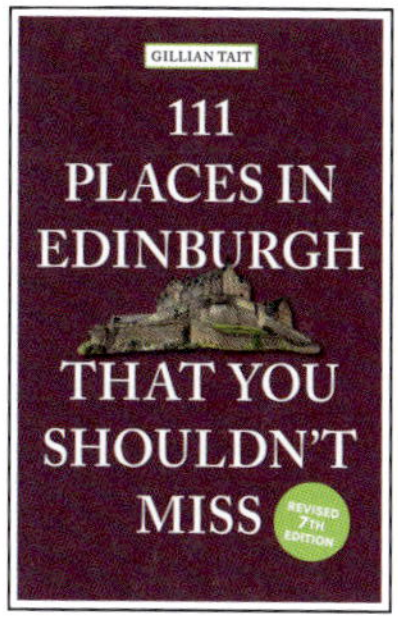

Gillian Tait
111 Places in Edinburgh That You Shouldn't Miss
ISBN 978-3-7408-2575-1

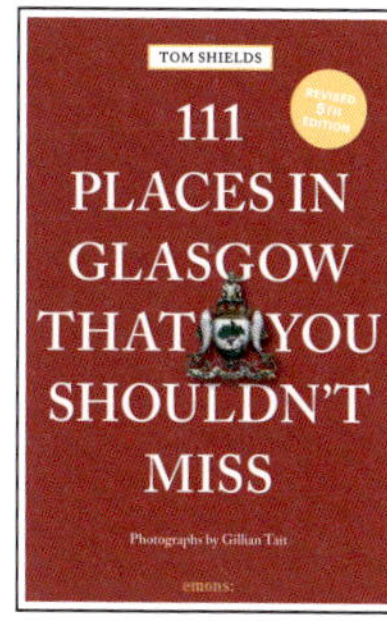

Tom Shields, Gillian Tait
111 Places in Glasgow That You Shouldn't Miss
ISBN 978-3-7408-2237-8

Gillian Tait
111 Places in Fife That You Shouldn't Miss
ISBN 978-3-7408-2806-6

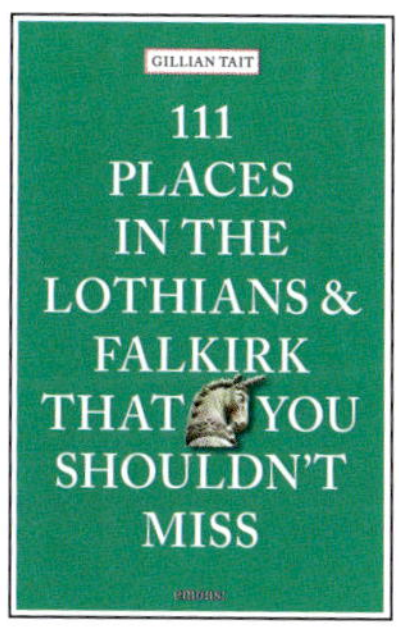

Gillian Tait
111 Places in the Lothians and Falkirk That You Shouldn't Miss
ISBN 978-3-7408-1569-1

David Taylor
111 Places in Newcastle That You Shouldn't Miss
ISBN 978-3-7408-1043-6

David Taylor
111 Places in Northumberland That You Shouldn't Miss
ISBN 978-3-7408-1792-3

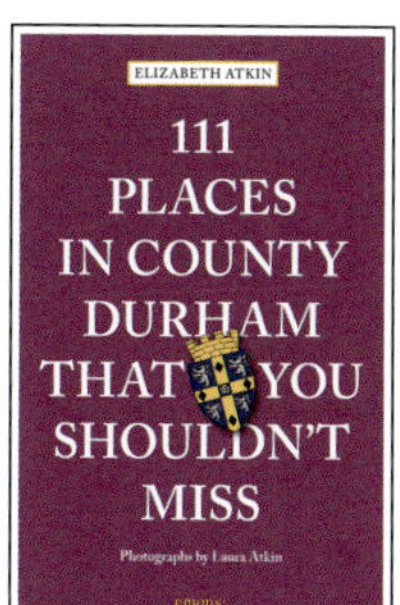

Elizabeth Atkin, Laura Atkin
111 Places in County Durham That You Shouldn't Miss
ISBN 978-3-7408-1426-7

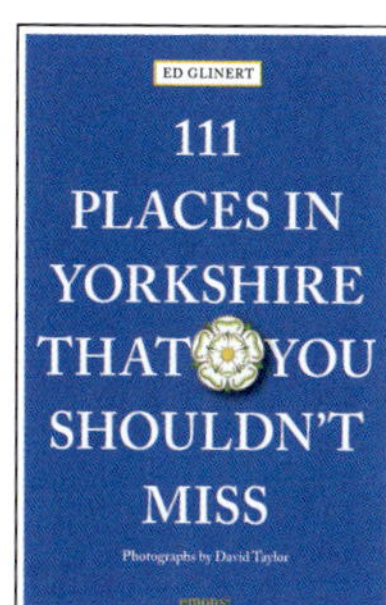

Ed Glinert, David Taylor
111 Places in Yorkshire That You Shouldn't Miss
ISBN 978-3-7408-1167-9

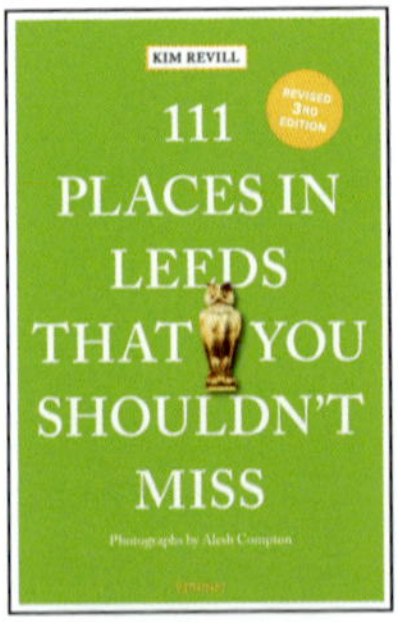

Kim Revill, Alesh Compton
111 Places in Leeds
That You Shouldn't Miss
ISBN 978-3-7408-2059-6

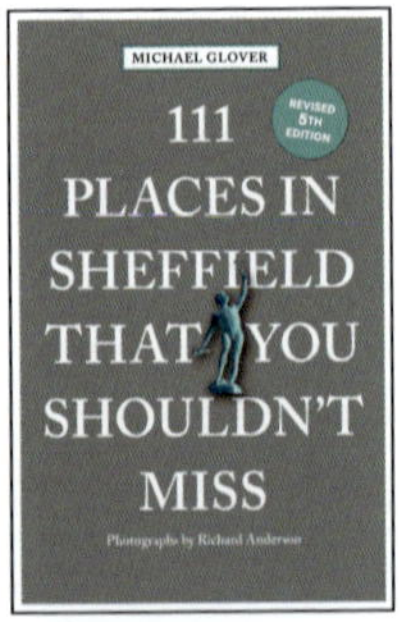

Michael Glover,
Richard Anderson
111 Places in Sheffield
That You Shouldn't Miss
ISBN 978-3-7408-2348-1

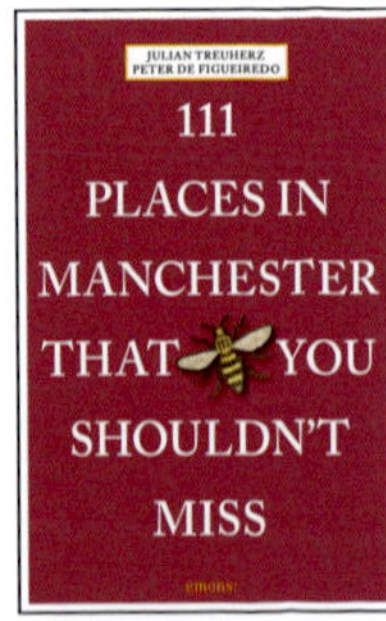

Julian Treuherz,
Peter de Figueiredo
111 Places in Manchester
That You Shouldn't Miss
ISBN 978-3-7408-2246-0

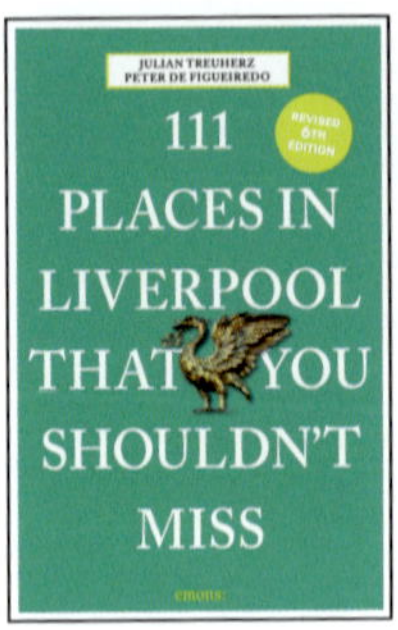

Julian Treuherz,
Peter de Figueiredo
111 Places in Liverpool
That You Shouldn't Miss
ISBN 978-3-7408-2515-7

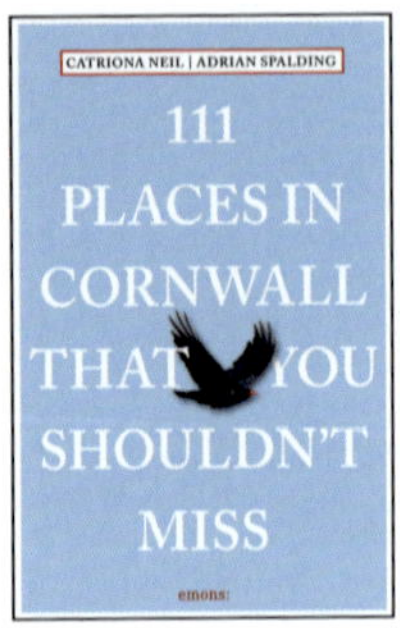

Catriona Neil, Adrian Spalding
111 Places in Cornwall
That You Shouldn't Miss
ISBN 978-3-7408-2805-9

Ed Glinert, Karin Tearle
111 Places in Essex
That You Shouldn't Miss
ISBN 978-3-7408-1593-6

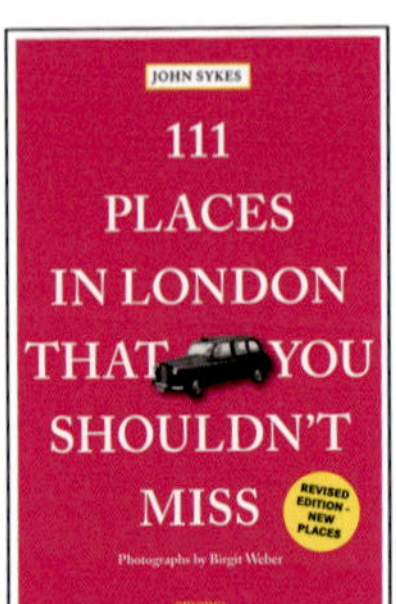

John Sykes, Birgit Weber
111 Places in London
That You Shouldn't Miss
ISBN 978-3-7408-2379-5

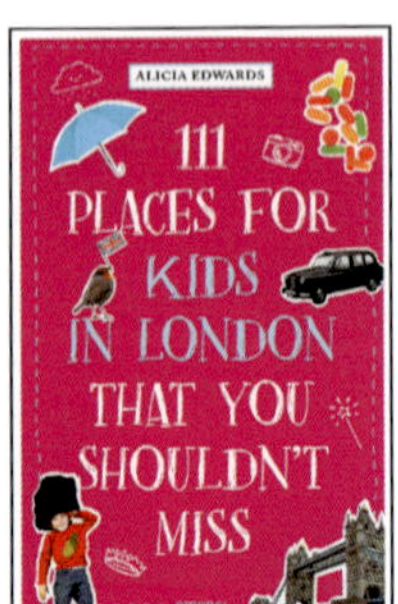

Alicia Edwards
111 Places for Kids in London
That You Shouldn't Miss
ISBN 978-3-7408-2196-8

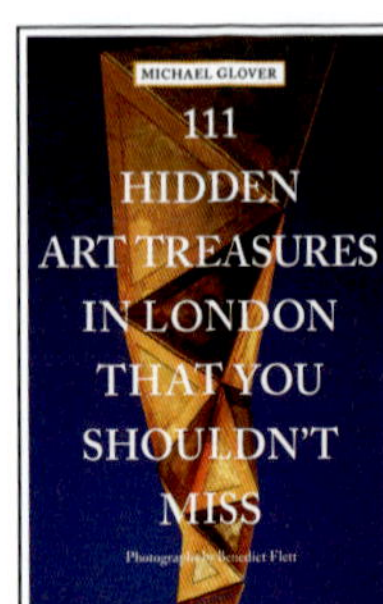

Michael Glover, Benedict Flett
111 Hidden Art Treasures
in London That You
Shouldn't Miss
ISBN 978-3-7408-1576-9

Julia Goodfellow Smith
111 Places in Swansea That You Shouldn't Miss
ISBN 978-3-7408-2065-7

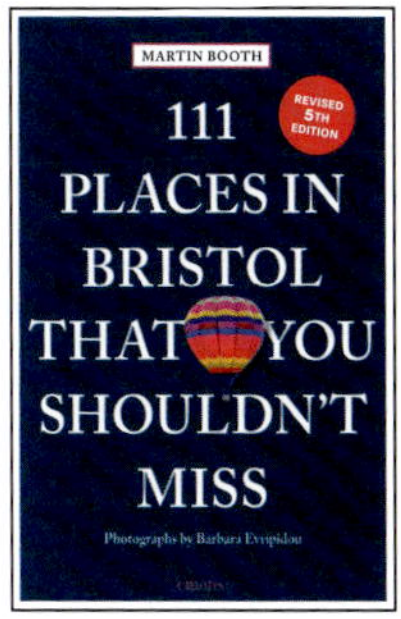

Martin Booth, Barbara Evripidou
111 Places in Bristol That You Shouldn't Miss
ISBN 978-3-7408-2512-6

Martin Booth, Barbara Evripidou
111 Places for Kids in Bristol That You Shouldn't Miss
ISBN 978-3-7408-1665-0

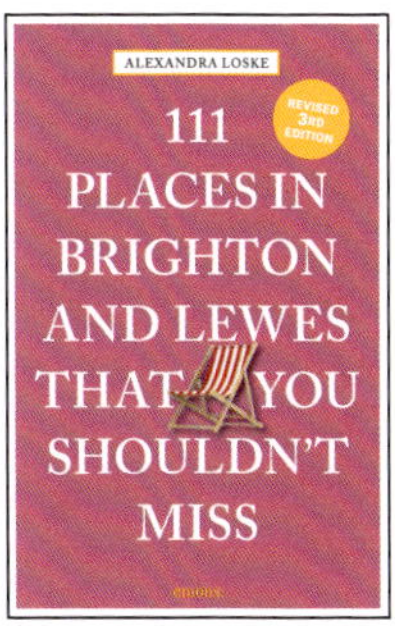

Alexandra Loske
111 Places in Brighton and Lewes That You Shouldn't Miss
ISBN 978-3-7408-1727-5

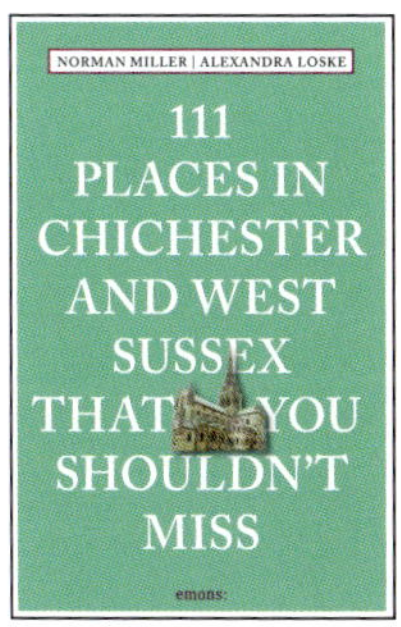

Norman Miller, Alexandra Loske
111 Places in Chichester and West Sussex That You Shouldn't Miss
ISBN 978-3-7408-2807-3

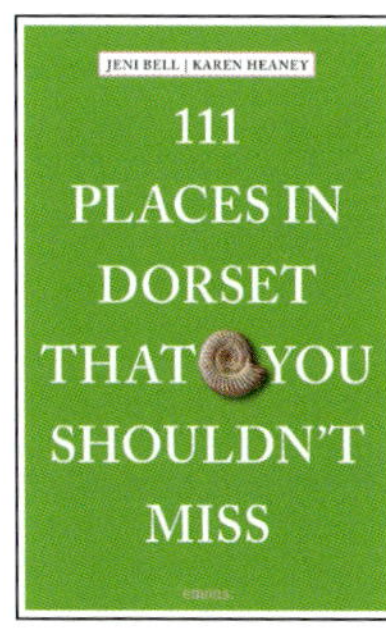

Jeni Bell, Karen Heaney
111 Places in Dorset That You Shouldn't Miss
ISBN 978-3-7408-2146-3

Katherine Bebo, Oliver Smith
111 Places in Bournemouth That You Shouldn't Miss
ISBN 978-3-7408-2646-8

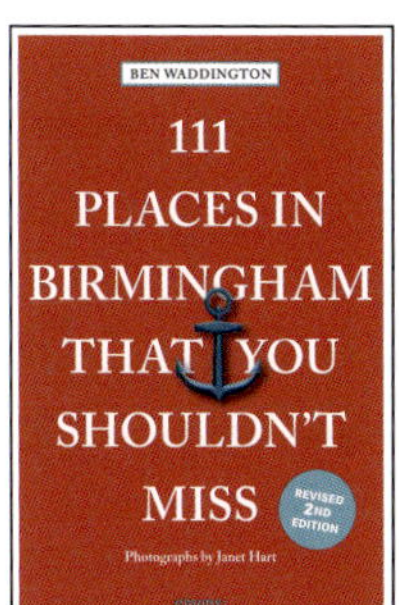

Ben Waddington, Janet Hart
111 Places in Birmingham That You Shouldn't Miss
ISBN 978-3-7408-2268-2

Solange Berchemin
111 Places in the Lake District That You Shouldn't Miss
ISBN 978-3-7408-2824-0

Photo Credits

© Photographs by Philip R. Stone, except:
Hermitage Castle (ch. 1), photo: Wirestock on freepik.com, CC-BY-4.0; Cultybraggan PoW Camp (ch. 10), photo: Wirestock on freepik.com, CC-BY-4.0; Curse of Patrick Hamilton (ch. 11), photo: rawpixel on freepik.com, CC-BY-4.0; The Tay Bridge Disaster (ch. 19), photo: Mateus Andre on freepik.com, CC-BY-4.0; Burn O'Vat (ch. 24), photo: Wirestock on freepik.com, CC-BY-4.0; The American Monument (ch. 25), photo: Wirestock on freepik.com, CC-BY-4.0; Badbea Clearance Village (ch. 26), photo: Wirestock.freepik.com, CC-BY-4.0; Cuween Chambered Cairn (ch. 30), photo: freepik.com, CC-BY-4.0; Eagle's Rock Memorial (ch. 31), photo: ninjason1 on freepik.com, CC-BY-4.0; The Gloup Disaster (ch. 35), photo: rawpixel on freepik.com, CC-BY-4.0; The Ghost Village (ch. 37), photo: freepik.com, CC-BY-4.0; Iolaire Memorial (ch. 39), photo: Wirestock on freepik.com, CC-BY-4.0; Royal Oak Memorial Garden (ch. 42), photo: Wirestock on freepik.com, CC-BY-4.0; Scapa Flow (ch. 44), photo: Wirestock on freepik.com, CC-BY-4.0; Canine Cemetery (ch. 54), photo: Wirestock on freepik.com, CC-BY-4.0; Inveraray Jail (ch. 95), photo: nickiabuida on freepik.com, CC-BY-4.0; A Lost Roman Legion (ch. 100), photo: freepik.com, CC-BY-4.0; Paisley Witches Memorial (ch. 103), photo: freepik.com, CC-BY-4.0; St Valentine's Bones (ch. 106), photo:freepik.com, CC-BY-4.0

Illustrative photos © Philip R. Stone
Image to illustrate Scotland's Secret Bunker (ch. 17); image to illustrate Sawney Bean's Cave (ch. 23); image to illustrate Flannan Isles Lighthouse (ch. 32); image to illustrate Flora MacDonald's Grave (ch. 36); image to illustrate Gruinard Island (ch. 38); image to illustrate Massacre Cave (ch. 40); image to illustrate The Unfinished Memorial (ch. 46); image to illustrate Dechmont UFO Monument (ch. 59); image to illustrate Mini-Submarine Wrecks (ch. 75); image to illustrate WWI Training Trenches (ch. 87); image to illustrate Still-

born Baby Memorial (ch. 107); image to illustrate Pierre's Unmarked Grave (ch. 104); image to illustrate Victoria Cross Memorial (photo shot within Glasgow Necropolis) (ch. 108); image to illustrate The Witch's Skull (ch. 110); image to illustrate Women of the Necropolis (photo shot within Glasgow Necropolis) (ch. 111)

Acknowledgements

Many people have contributed to this book. Thank you to Rachael Dorrian, who has lovingly supported me throughout and accompanied me on a photography adventure to Scotland. Thank you also to my daughter and son, Sara and Aaron, who patiently listened to my many tales of 'victims and villains' featured in this book. Thanks also to Scott Hartles who helped me steady myself against wind and sea while photographing at Crammond Island. My colleagues at the Institute of Creativity, Communities and Culture (ICCC) at the University of Lancashire (UK) deserve thanks for providing research funding that ensured much of my photography. My gratitude to Rosalind Horton (Cambridge Editorial) for her diligent and prompt editing of manuscript drafts, and for spotting my erroneous inclusion of night buses in 'Getting there'. I am grateful to everyone at Emons, particularly Laura Olk, who publish my words and pictures. Finally, a big shout out to Karen Seiger (Sirene MediaWorks), who first offered me the opportunity to write about 111 dark places.
Grātiam habeō.

Philip R. Stone, Ph.D. is an internationally recognised Professor specialising in dark tourism and difficult heritage. He has extensively published academic literature on these subjects and has presented his research at conferences worldwide. Additionally, Philip serves as a media consultant on dark tourism, with notable clients including the BBC, CNN, *The New York Times, The Guardian* and *The Washington Post*. He is the author of the pioneering book *111 Dark Places in England That You Shouldn't Miss*.